Helen Harden

Cambridge IGCSE®
Chemistry Maths Skills

Workbook

First Edition

CAMBRIDGE UNIVERSITY PRESS

CAMBRIDGE
UNIVERSITY PRESS

University Printing House, Cambridge CB2 8BS, United Kingdom

One Liberty Plaza, 20th Floor, New York, NY 10006, USA

477 Williamstown Road, Port Melbourne, VIC 3207, Australia

314–321, 3rd Floor, Plot 3, Splendor Forum, Jasola District Centre, New Delhi – 110025, India

79 Anson Road, #06-04/06, Singapore 079906

Cambridge University Press is part of the University of Cambridge.

It furthers the University's mission by disseminating knowledge in the pursuit of education, learning and research at the highest international levels of excellence.

Information on this title: www.cambridge.org

© Cambridge University Press 2018

This publication is in copyright. Subject to statutory exception and to the provisions of relevant collective licensing agreements, no reproduction of any part may take place without the written permission of Cambridge University Press.

First published 2018

20 19 18 17 16 15 14 13 12 11 10 9 8 7 6 5 4 3 2 1

Printed in Spain by GraphyCems

A catalogue record for this publication is available from the British Library

ISBN 978-1-108-72813-3

Additional resources for this publication at cambridge.org/9781108728133

Cambridge University Press has no responsibility for the persistence or accuracy of URLs for external or third-party internet websites referred to in this publication, and does not guarantee that any content on such websites is, or will remain, accurate or appropriate. Information regarding prices, travel timetables, and other factual information given in this work is correct at the time of first printing but Cambridge University Press does not guarantee the accuracy of such information thereafter.

....

NOTICE TO TEACHERS IN THE UK
It is illegal to reproduce any part of this work in material form (including photocopying and electronic storage) except under the following circumstances:
(i) where you are abiding by a licence granted to your school or institution by the Copyright Licensing Agency;
(ii) where no such licence exists, or where you wish to exceed the terms of a licence, and you have gained the written permission of Cambridge University Press;
(iii) where you are allowed to reproduce without permission under the provisions of Chapter 3 of the Copyright, Designs and Patents Act 1988, which covers, for example, the reproduction of short passages within certain types of educational anthology and reproduction for the purpose of setting examination questions.

....

All exam-style questions and sample answers in this title were written by the authors. In examinations, the way marks are awarded may be different.

Contents

Introduction iv

Chapter 1: Representing values 2
Maths focus 1: Using units 2
Maths focus 2: Understanding very large and very small numbers 6
Maths focus 3: Writing numbers in a required form 11

Chapter 2: Working with data 17
Maths focus 1: Collecting data 17
Maths focus 2: Understanding types of data 22
Maths focus 3: Recording and processing data 25

Chapter 3: Drawing charts and graphs 35
Maths focus 1: Drawing bar charts 35
Maths focus 2: Drawing pie charts 40
Maths focus 3: Drawing line graphs 46

Chapter 4: Interpreting data 63
Maths focus 1: Interpreting charts 64
Maths focus 2: Reading values from a line graph 69
Maths focus 3: Interpreting the shape of line graphs 72

Chapter 5: Doing calculations 85
Maths focus 1: Using basic maths operations in calculations 85
Maths focus 2: Calculating percentages 89
Maths focus 3: Using mathematical formulae in calculations (Supplement) 91
Maths focus 4: Calculating using ratios 98

Chapter 6: Working with shape 106
Maths focus 1: Comparing surface area and volume 106

Additional questions involving several maths skills 114

The Periodic Table 118

Glossary 119

Acknowledgements 121

Introduction

This workbook has been written to help you to improve your skills in the mathematical processes that you need in your Cambridge IGCSE Chemistry course. The exercises will guide you and give you practice in:

- representing values
- working with data
- drawing charts and graphs
- interpreting data
- doing calculations
- working with shape.

Each chapter focuses on several maths skills that you need to master to be successful in your Chemistry course and explains why you need these skills. Then, for each skill, there is a step-by-step worked example of a question that involves the skill. This is followed by practice questions for you to try. These are not like exam questions. They are designed to develop your skills and understanding. They get increasingly challenging. Tips are often given alongside to guide you. Spaces, lines or graph grids are provided for your answers.

It is best to work through Chapters 1 and 2 early in your course, as they will help to ensure that you have a secure understanding of number and units, as well as confidence in reading scales when making measurements. Chapter 3 shows you the skills you need to draw a variety of different types of chart and graph. These chapters will support you with many practical activities that you may carry out.

Chapter 4 covers the skills needed to read information from charts and graphs, as well as the specific graph skills that you will need when studying rates of reaction. Chapter 6 shows you the mathematics of the ratio of surface area : volume, which will help to explain why changing surface area affects the rate of reaction.

A few of the maths concepts and skills are only needed if you are following the Extended syllabus (Core plus Supplement). The headings of these sections are marked 'Supplement'. In other areas just one or two of the practice questions may be based on the Supplement syllabus content, and these are also clearly marked. Most of these are in Chapter 5, which covers the key calculations needed in chemistry, including the use of moles (Supplement only).

There are further questions at the end of each chapter for you to try, to give you more confidence in using the skills practised within the chapter. At the end of the book there are additional questions that may require any of the maths skills from all of the chapters.

You will find a copy of the Periodic Table at the end of the book. You will need this to look up relative atomic masses for some questions.

Important mathematical terms are printed in **bold** type and these are explained in the glossary at the back of the book.

Representing values

Why do you need to represent values in chemistry?

- If you want to communicate measurements in chemistry, you will need to record values that you measure. You must make sure that another person will be able to understand your measurements, so how you represent them is important. As well as the numerical value, you must also include the correct **unit**.
- In chemistry, you will need to understand numbers that are much larger or much smaller than numbers you may be used to working with. Writing these numbers in different ways will make them easier to understand and compare.

Maths focus 1: Using units

All units of measure in general use are based upon *Standard International (SI) units*.

Table 1.1 shows some SI units that you may meet in chemistry.

Quantity	Unit	SI abbreviation
length	metre	m
mass	kilogram	kg
time	second	s
amount of substance	mole*	mol

Table 1.1: SI units for common quantities
Supplement only.

In chemistry the SI unit for temperature is the kelvin, but it may be easier to use the Celsius **scale**, on which the freezing point of water is 0 °C and the boiling point of water (at 1 atmosphere pressure) is 100 °C. This is more useful for many laboratory measurements, although the kelvin scale is used in more advanced chemistry studies. Note that a temperature difference in kelvin, such as 30 kelvin, is the same as a temperature difference of 30 degrees on the Celsius scale.

> **TIP**
> Remember that a temperature can take a negative value on the Celsius scale.

What maths skills do you need to be able to use units?

1	Choosing the correct unit	• Identify the type of quantity that the apparatus measures • Select an appropriate unit for that quantity
2	Writing the unit symbol	• Recall or look up the unit symbol • Check whether the unit requires index notation, for example, cm^2, cm^3
3	Writing symbols for derived units	• Work out how the quantity is calculated • Write the derived units to be consistent with the calculation

Chapter 1: Representing values

Maths skills practice

How does using units help to communicate values measured during chemical reactions?

When you are carrying out experimental work in chemistry, it is essential that you use the appropriate units to record and communicate any measurements you take.

For example, it is meaningless to state the volume of gas produced during a chemical reaction simply as '16'. Using units clearly specifies the volume measured. For example, a volume of 16 cm^3 is completely different from a volume of 16 litres. Similarly, recording the mass of product formed in an experiment as '3' means nothing unless you add the correct units, such as grams. Remember that an amount of 3 g is a thousand times smaller than 3 kg, so it is essential to use the correct prefix as well as the correct unit.

Most values used in chemistry require units as they are measures of particular quantities, such as length, mass, temperature, time, volume or the amount of a substance.

Maths skill 1: Choosing the correct unit

It is important that you can name the units commonly used in chemistry measurements.

> **WATCH OUT**
>
> Not all values require units. Relative atomic mass gives the average mass of naturally occurring atoms of an element, based on a scale in which the carbon-12 atom has a mass of exactly 12 units. For example, the relative atomic mass of hydrogen is 1, meaning that, on average, atoms of hydrogen have a mass that is $\frac{1}{12}$ the mass of a carbon atom. This is a **ratio** and therefore it needs no units.

> **LINK**
>
> See Chapter 5 for more on ratios.

> **TIP**
>
> Make sure that the units are also appropriate to the scale on the measuring apparatus. A small beaker will not measure litres.

WORKED EXAMPLE 1

Choose the correct unit of measurement associated with this small beaker.

A centimetres **B** litres **C** square centimetres **D** cubic centimetres

Step 1 Identify the type of quantity that the apparatus measures.

A beaker measures volume.

Step 2 Select an appropriate unit for that quantity.

> **KEY QUESTIONS TO ASK YOURSELF:**
>
> - What units are used to measure this type of quantity?
>   Volume may be measured in a variety of units including litres (l) or cubic centimetres (cm^3).
> - Which units are appropriate for the scale on the measuring equipment?
>   A small beaker will not measure litres. The scale is likely to be in cubic centimetres (cm^3).

So appropriate units in this case are cubic centimetres.

Cambridge IGCSE Chemistry Maths Skills

Practice question 1

Draw lines to match each item of measuring apparatus with the appropriate unit of measurement.

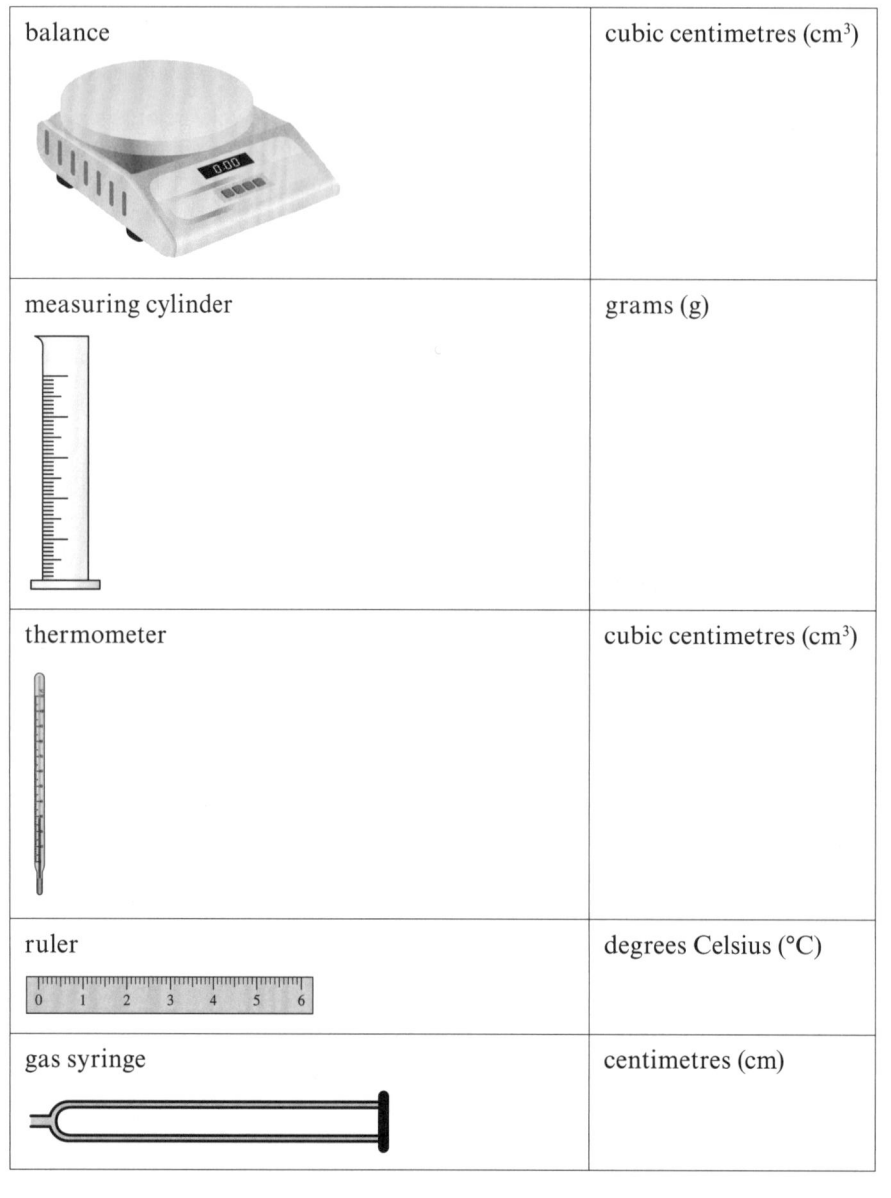

balance	cubic centimetres (cm^3)
measuring cylinder	grams (g)
thermometer	cubic centimetres (cm^3)
ruler	degrees Celsius (°C)
gas syringe	centimetres (cm)

> **WATCH OUT**
> Some unit symbols (abbreviated units) start with a capital letter. This occurs when they are named after a person who invented them; for example, the Celsius temperature is named after the Swedish astronomer Anders Celsius, who developed a similar temperature scale. Most unit symbols start with a lower case letter.

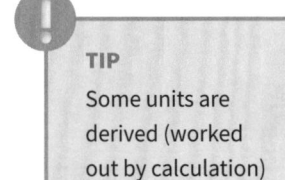

Maths skill 2: Writing the unit symbol

Units are not usually written out in full. Each unit has a short form, or abbreviation, comprising 1–3 letters.

> **TIP**
> Some units are derived (worked out by calculation) from SI units.

Quantity	Unit	Abbreviation
length	metres	m
mass	kilograms	kg
time	seconds	s
temperature	degrees Celsius	°C
*amount of substance**	*mole*	mol

Table 1.2 Abbreviations for some SI units
Supplement only.

> **LINK**
> See Chapter 5.

Chapter 1: Representing values

LINK
See Maths focus 2, Maths skills 3 'Understanding unit prefixes'.

TIP
Always remember to include the correct index or **power** when necessary. It is incorrect to write a volume of liquid as 10 cm because centimetres measure length.

Other units are created by inserting a prefix in front of the SI unit. Centimetres are used for measuring shorter distances than metres, for example: 1 cm is $\frac{1}{100}$ or 0.01 m.

Some units require **index** notation. For example:

- **Area** is always measured in *square* units (such as m^2 or cm^2), since it is obtained by multiplying two lengths, for example, m × m or cm × cm (think about counting squares on a grid to find areas).

- **Volume** is always measured in *cubic* units (such as m^3 or cm^3), since it is obtained by multiplying three lengths, for example, m × m × m, or cm × cm × cm (think about counting cubes in a cuboid made from unit cubes).

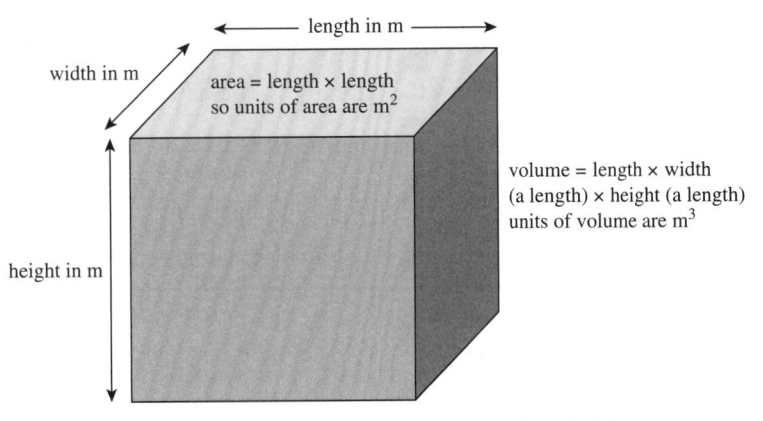

Figure 1.1 Comparing area of a face and volume of a cuboid

WORKED EXAMPLE 2

The length and width of a piece of paper have been measured in centimetres. Write down the correct unit symbol for its area.

Step 1 Recall or look up the unit symbol.

In this case it is centimetres (cm).

Step 2 Check whether the unit requires index notation.

Area is found by multiplying length by width so it must be measured in square units.

The unit is square centimetres (cm^2).

Practice question 2

Write down the correct unit symbol for each measurement.

a Mass of copper sulfate, measured on a digital balance that measures in grams ....

b Temperature of water, measured using a thermometer marked in degrees Celsius ....

c Time taken for a reaction to take place, measured using a stopwatch that displays seconds ....

d Length of magnesium ribbon, measured using a ruler marked in centimetres ....

e Area of floor in a laboratory, where the length and width are measured in metres ....

f Volume of liquid in a beaker that measures in cubic centimetres ....

Cambridge IGCSE Chemistry Maths Skills

> **TIP**
> The solidus (/) symbol indicates 'per', or division.

> **WATCH OUT**
> The symbol / is also used as a separator between a variable name and its unit, in tables and on graphs. Here, you read the / sign as 'in', so 'Temperature / °C' means 'temperature in degrees Celsius'.

Maths skill 3: Writing symbols for derived units

The units for some quantities are derived (based on a calculation) from other units. For example, you can calculate the **rate** of a reaction by dividing the volume of gas produced by the time taken, rather like calculating the speed of a car by dividing the distance travelled by time taken. If the volume is measured in cubic centimetres and the time in seconds, the units of rate of reaction are cm^3/s (cubic centimetres per second).

WORKED EXAMPLE 3

You can work out the density of an aluminium cube by dividing its mass (in grams) by its volume (in cubic centimetres).

Write down the correct derived unit for density.

Step 1 Work out how the quantity is calculated.

The calculation for density is: $\dfrac{mass}{volume}$

Step 2 Write the derived units to be consistent with the calculation.

The derived units are grams per cubic centimetre (g/cm^3).

Practice question 3

Write down the correct derived unit for each calculated quantity:

a   The rate of a reaction (how fast a reaction takes place), calculated by dividing the mass of product made (in grams) by the time taken (in seconds) ....

b   The density of a bronze statue, calculated by dividing the mass of the statue (in kilograms) by its volume (in cubic metres) ....

c   The rate of a reaction, calculated by dividing the volume of gas produced (in cubic centimetres) by the time taken (in seconds) ....

Maths focus 2: Understanding very large and very small numbers

In chemistry you need to understand very large numbers.

In 12 g of carbon there are about **602 000 000 000 000 000 000 000** atoms.

You also need to understand very small numbers.

A single carbon atom has a **diameter** of about 0.000 000 000 17 m.

It is very important to use the correct number of zeros. The value of the number depends upon the place value of the digits. If you use the wrong number of zeros, the value of the number will change.

However, writing out this many zeros takes a lot of time so very large and very small numbers are often written using **powers of ten** instead.

The number of atoms in 12 g of carbon can also be written as 6.02×10^{23}.

The diameter of a carbon atom can be written as 1.7×10^{-10} m.

Sometimes in chemistry the units are changed for very large and very small numbers by adding a **prefix** such as kilo (k) or nano (n). These prefixes replace the power of ten.

So $3 \text{ kg} = 3 \times 10^3 \text{ g}$ or 3000 g.

Chapter 1: Representing values

What maths skills do you need to be able to understand very large and very small numbers?

1	Understanding place value	• Compare digits with the highest place value
		• Compare digits with the next highest place values
2	Understanding powers of ten	• Write out the multiplication
		• Calculate the number as it would be written in full
3	Understanding unit prefixes	• Write the measurement in terms of a power of ten
		• Calculate the number as it would be written in full

Maths skills practice

How does understanding very large and very small numbers help to improve your understanding of the size and number of different particles?

Some numbers used in chemistry are so large, or so small, that they are difficult to imagine. Writing these in a clearer way, such as using powers of ten or prefixes, helps to understand how the size of different particles compare. A particle of PM2.5 'particulate' air pollution has a diameter of about 2.5×10^{-6} m or 2.5 µm, whereas a PM10 particle is about 10×10^{-6} m or 10 µm in diameter.

Understanding powers of ten and **unit prefixes** means that you will instantly know that these are much larger than a typical atom, which is about 1×10^{-10} m in diameter.

Before you can do this, though, it is important that you have a good understanding of place value in numbers that are written out in full.

Maths skill 1: Understanding place value

The position of a digit in a number determines its place value. The left-most digit in a number has the highest place value.

For example, the number in Table 1.3 (reading from left to right) is:

three hundred and twenty-three billion, four hundred and fifty-six million, three hundred and forty-five thousand, six hundred and forty-seven

Hundreds of billions, 10^{11}	Tens of billions, 10^{10}	Billions, 10^9	Hundreds of millions, 10^8	Tens of millions, 10^7	Millions, 10^6	Hundreds of thousands, 10^5	Tens of thousands, 10^4	Thousands, 10^3	Hundreds, 10^2	Tens, 10^1	Units, 10^0
3	2	3	4	5	6	3	4	5	6	4	7

Table 1.3 Place values for large numbers

The decimal fraction in Table 1.4 is one billionth.

	Tenths	Hundredths	Thousandths	Ten-thousandths	Hundred-thousandths	Millionths	Ten-millionths	Hundred-millionths	Billionths
0.	0	0	0	0	0	0	0	0	1

Table 1.4 Place values for small numbers

Cambridge IGCSE Chemistry Maths Skills

TIP

Read the number from left to right. The place value of the first non-zero number helps you decide how big the number is.

WORKED EXAMPLE 4

Find the largest number in the following list.

A 7 242 519   B 8 143 921   C 8 349 321   D 924 107

Step 1 Compare digits with the highest place value.

A, B and C all have millions as the highest place value. B and C both have digits showing 8 million, so are larger than A, which has 7 million.

Step 2 Compare digits with the next highest place values.

The next highest place value is hundreds of thousands. B has 1 hundred thousand but C has 3 hundred thousand. So the largest number is C.

Practice question 4

Circle the *largest* number in each list.

a 674 591   92 342   141 294   692 381

b 1 943 986   1 949 789   1 942 987   1 944 098

c 0.09   0.12   0.17   0.06

d 0.09   0.015   0.026   0.07

e 0.000 007 2   0.000 008 5   0.000 000 1   0.000 000 165

TIP

Look for the first non-zero digit and use place value to compare numbers.

Practice question 5

Circle the *smallest* number in each list.

a 1 232 452   123 532   723 453   115 362

b 0.123 451   0.345 984   0.135 034   0.124 093

c 0.000 002 234 0.000 002   0.000 002 4   0.000 002 34

d 234.56   234.25   232.12   232.013 4

e 104 985.99   110 374.12   104 895.99   104 895.82

Maths skill 2: Understanding powers of ten

Powers of 10 are the result of multiplying 10 by itself.

A negative power of any number is the **reciprocal** of the corresponding positive power. This means, for example, that $10^{-1} = \frac{1}{10}$, or $1 \div 10$ (the reciprocal of 10).

Chapter 1: Representing values

$10^1 = 10$	$10^{-1} = \frac{1}{10}$ or 0.1
$10^2 = 10 \times 10 = 100$	$10^{-2} = \frac{1}{10 \times 10} = \frac{1}{100}$ or $1 \div 10 \div 10 = 0.01$
$10^5 = 10 \times 10 \times 10 \times 10 \times 10 = 100\,000$	$10^{-5} = \frac{1}{10 \times 10 \times 10 \times 10 \times 10} = \frac{1}{100\,000}$ $= 1 \div 10 \div 10 \div 10 \div 10 \div 10$ or 0.00001

Table 1.5 Powers of ten

Very large and very small numbers are often recorded as multiples of powers of ten. This saves having to write out lots of zeros.

For example: $4 \times 10^3 = 4 \times 10 \times 10 \times 10 = 4000$

So multiplying by 10^3 means that you need to multiply by 10 three times.

In general 4×10^n means that 4 is multiplied by 10 n times.

4×10^1	4×10	40
4×10^2	$4 \times 10 \times 10$	400
4×10^3	$4 \times 10 \times 10 \times 10$	4000
4×10^4	$4 \times 10 \times 10 \times 10 \times 10$	40 000
4×10^5	$4 \times 10 \times 10 \times 10 \times 10 \times 10$	400 000
4×10^6	$4 \times 10 \times 10 \times 10 \times 10 \times 10 \times 10$	4 000 000

Table 1.6 Multiplying by powers of ten

Multiplying a number by a negative power of ten tells you how many times to divide it by ten.

For example: $4 \times 10^{-3} = 4 \times \frac{1}{10 \times 10 \times 10} = 4 \div 10 \div 10 \div 10$

WORKED EXAMPLE 5 (POSITIVE POWERS OF TEN)

Write 5×10^5 in full.

Step 1 Write out the multiplication.

$5 \times 10^5 = 5 \times 10 \times 10 \times 10 \times 10 \times 10$

Step 2 Calculate the number as it would be written in full.

$= 5 \times 100\,000$

$= 500\,000$

Practice question 6

These numbers are expressed as multiples of powers of ten. Write them in full.

a 3×10^3 ....

b 45×10^6 ....

c 4×10^1 ....

d 123×10^{10} ....

Cambridge IGCSE Chemistry Maths Skills

WORKED EXAMPLE 6 (NEGATIVE POWERS OF TEN)

Write 3×10^{-4} as a decimal.

Step 1 Write out the multiplication.

$$3 \times 10^{-4} = 3 \times \frac{1}{10 \times 10 \times 10 \times 10} = 3 \div 10 \div 10 \div 10 \div 10$$

Step 2 Calculate the number as it would be written in full.

$$= 3 \times 0.0001 = 0.0003$$

Practice question 7

Write each of these negative powers of ten as a decimal.

a 2×10^{-2} ....

b 34×10^{-6} ....

c 9×10^{-9} ....

d 43×10^{-5} ....

Maths skill 3: Understanding unit prefixes

Very often in science rather than writing a number either in full or using powers of ten, you can just change the unit by using a prefix.

The prefix tells you the power of ten by which to multiply the measurement to find the full number.

For example: 7 kg means $7 \times 10^3 = 7000$ g

Table 1.7 shows some prefixes you should know.

Unit prefix	Unit prefix symbol	Multiplying factor	Example unit names	Example unit symbols
kilo-	k	10^3	kilogram	kg
deci-	d	10^{-1}	cubic decimetre	dm^3
centi-	c	10^{-2}	cubic centimetre	cm^3
milli-	m	10^{-3}	milligram	mg
			millimetre	mm
micro-	μ	10^{-6}	microgram	μg
nano-	n	10^{-9}	nanometre	nm

Table 1.7 Prefixes used with common measures

Chapter 1: Representing values

LINK

See Maths skill 2 'Understanding powers of ten'.

WORKED EXAMPLE 7

Write 8 mg without using the prefix.

Step 1 Write the measurement in terms of a power of ten.

$8\,\text{mg} = 8 \times 10^{-3}\,\text{g}$

Step 2 Calculate the number as it would be written in full.

$8 \times 10^{-3} = 8 \times \dfrac{1}{10 \times 10 \times 10} = 8 \div 10 \div 10 \div 10 = 0.008$

So $8\,\text{mg} = 8 \times 10^{-3}\,\text{g} = 0.008\,\text{g}$

Practice question 8

Write each measurement without the prefix.

- **a** i 3 mg ....
- ii 4 µg ....
- iii 3 kg ....
- **b** i 4 mm ....
- ii 2 cm ....
- iii 7 nm ....
- **c** i 4 cm ....
- ii 2 dm ....

Practice question 9

Write each measurement without the prefix.

- **a** i 42 mg ....
- ii 402 µg ....
- iii 345 kg ....
- **b** i 74 nm ....
- ii 7.4 nm ....
- iii 704 nm ....

Maths focus 3: Writing numbers in a required form

Sometimes in chemistry you are required to write a number in a particular form.

When very large or very small numbers are expressed in terms of a power of ten, the convention is to use a system called **standard form** or **standard index form.**

A number in standard form is expressed as a number greater than or equal to 1 but less than 10 multiplied by a power of ten. For example, 54 000 can be written as 5.4×10^4. However, 54×10^3 is *not* in standard form because 54 is not between 1 and 10.

The results of calculations should be rounded to an appropriate number of **significant figures**, based upon the lowest number of significant figures of the numbers used in the calculation.

Cambridge IGCSE Chemistry Maths Skills

What maths skills do you need to be able to understand very large and very small numbers?

1	Writing numbers in standard form	• Write the digits as a number that is greater than or equal to 1 and less than 10
		• Work out how many times you have to multiply or divide the number by 10 to get back to your original number
		• Write the number, using the correct power of ten
2	Writing numbers to the required number of significant figures (sf)	• Identify the correct number of significant figures
		• Decide whether to round up or down.

Maths skills practice

How does writing numbers in a required form help communicate chemistry?

Standard form provides a consistent system for communicating and comparing very small and large numbers. The power of ten gives a useful **estimate** of the size of the number.

It is important that all values in chemistry are recorded to an appropriate number of significant figures. Writing the result of a calculation as $34.938\,475\,cm^3$ when in reality the measurements used in the calculation were only to three significant figures suggests a much greater degree of **accuracy** than was actually achieved in the experiment. It is better to write the number to three significant figures, that is $34.9\,cm^3$.

Maths skill 1: Writing numbers in standard form

A number in standard form always includes a number that is greater than or equal to 1 and less than 10 multiplied by a power of ten.

So for the number 4 060 000:

- 4.06×10^6 is correctly in standard form because 4.06 is between 1 and 10.
- 406×10^4 is in index form, but is *not* in standard form because 406 is greater than 10.

> **TIP**
> In standard form the decimal point always comes after the most significant figure.

> **LINK**
> See Maths skill 2, 'Writing numbers to the required number of significant figures (sf).'

> **TIP**
> Note that calculators differ, so you need to know the correct key on the calculator that you use.

Standard form on your calculator

Calculators do not all work in the same way, so you must make sure you know how to use yours. This is especially important when you need to enter or read numbers in standard form. This may involve using the E key (or the [EE] key).

For example, to enter 1.67×10^{11}, a typical key sequence would be:

1.67   E11

The screen would show the number as:

$1.67\ 10^{11}$

WORKED EXAMPLE 8

12 g of carbon contains 6.02×10^{23} carbon atoms.

Use your calculator to work out how many carbon atoms there are in 24 g of carbon.

$2 \times 6.02 \times 10^{23} = 1.20 \times 10^{24}$

Chapter 1: Representing values

WORKED EXAMPLE 9 (LARGE NUMBERS)

Write 5 400 000 in standard form.

Step 1 Rewrite the non-zero digits as a number that is greater than or equal to 1 and less than 10.

5.4

Step 2 Work out how many times you have to multiply this number by 10 to get back to your original number.

5.4 must be multiplied by 10 six times (5.4 × 10 × 10 × 10 × 10 × 10 × 10) to reach 5 400 000.

5   4   0   0   0   0   0   .   0
                            5   .   4
× 10 × 10 × 10 × 10 × 10 × 10

Step 3 Write the number, using the correct power of ten.

$5.4 \times 10 \times 10 \times 10 \times 10 \times 10 \times 10 = 5.4 \times 10^6$

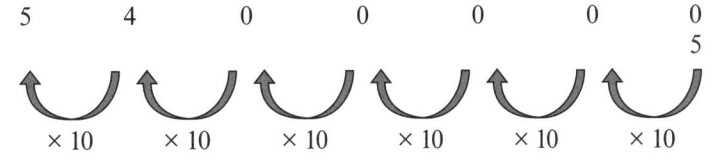

TIP

If there are significant zeros between the digits in a number, these must appear in the number written in standard form, for example: $3\,050\,000 = 3.05 \times 10^6$

Practice question 10

Write these numbers in standard form.

a 134 000 ....

b 103 000 ....

c 120 000 000 ....

d 140 ....

Practice question 11

Write these values in standard form.

a 34 000 000 000 000 carbon atoms ....

b 142 000 g ....

c 145 m^3 ....

The method for converting very small numbers into standard form is slightly different.

WORKED EXAMPLE 10 (SMALL NUMBERS)

Write 0.000 0012 in standard form.

Step 1 Rewrite the non-zero digits as a number that is greater or equal to 1 and less than 10.

1.2

Step 2 Work out how many times you have to divide this number by 10 to get back to your original number.

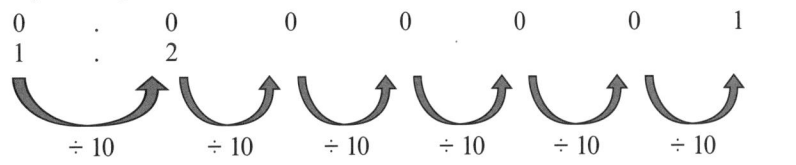

0   .   0   0   0   0   0   1   2
1   .   2
÷ 10 ÷ 10 ÷ 10 ÷ 10 ÷ 10 ÷ 10

Step 3 Write the number, using the correct power of ten.

$1.2 \div 10 \div 10 \div 10 \div 10 \div 10 \div 10 = 1.2 \times \dfrac{1}{10 \times 10 \times 10 \times 10 \times 10 \times 10} = 1.2 \times 10^{-6}$

Cambridge IGCSE Chemistry Maths Skills

Practice question 12

Write these numbers in standard form.

a 0.0034 ....

b 0.000 005 4 ....

c 0.000 507 ....

d 0. 000 000 009 754 ....

Practice question 13

Write these measurements in standard form.

a 0.000 000 000 15 m ....

b 0.003 g ....

c 0.000 000 023 g ....

d 0.0009 m^3 ....

Maths skill 2: Writing numbers to the required number of significant figures (sf)

The rules for **rounding** to a given number of significant figures are similar to those for rounding to the nearest ten or hundred or to a given number of decimal places. The significant figures in a number are counted from the first non-zero digit.

WORKED EXAMPLE 11

Write 124 321 correct to two significant figures.

Step 1 Identify the correct number of significant figures.

The first two significant figures are the first and second digits in the number, which have the two highest place values. These are the two digits on the left of the digit to be rounded.

1st sf   2nd sf
 ↓   ↓
 1   2   4   3   2   1

Step 2 Decide whether to round up or down.

Look at the digit in the third significant place.

If it is 0, 1, 2, 3 or 4, leave the first two digits as they are and replace all the rest of the digits in the number with zero.

If it is 5, 6, 7, 8 or 9, increase the digit in the second place by 1 and replace all the rest of the digits in the number with zero.

The next digit is 4 so round down, giving 120 000.

TIP

If there is a zero between non-zero digits, for example, 207 224, this counts as a significant figure.

Chapter 1: Representing values

WORKED EXAMPLE 12

Write 0.267 93 correct to two significant figures.

Step 1 Identify the correct number of significant figures.

Identify the first two significant figures. The third is the one to be rounded.

```
        1st sf    2nd sf
          ↓         ↓
0.        2         6      7     9     3
```

Step 2 Decide whether to round up or down.

Look at the digit in the next place.

The next digit is 7 so round up, giving 0.27.

Practice question 14

a There are 423 912 atoms in an amount. Round this to:

   i 1 sf   ....

   ii 3 sf   ....

b Round a mass of 0.324 g to:

   i 1 sf   ....

   ii 2 sf   ....

c There are 1 064 126 atoms in an amount. Round this to:

   i 2 sf   ....

   ii 3 sf   ....

d Round a mass of 0.407 312 g to:

   i 1 sf   ....

   ii 2 sf   ....

Further questions

1 Insert the correct unit prefixes (k, m, µ, c) into each statement.

Each prefix is used only once.

   a The diameter of a gold coin is 3 ..... m.

   b The thickness of a gold ring is 3 ..... m.

   c The mass of a gold bar is 12.4 ..... g.

   d The thickness of gold leaf (sheet) is 0.1 ..... m.

Cambridge IGCSE Chemistry Maths Skills

2 12 g of carbon is placed in a beaker. This contains 6.02×10^{23} atoms of carbon.

   a Another 12 g of carbon is added to the beaker.

     Calculate the number of atoms of carbon now in the beaker.

     Write this answer in standard form.

     ....

     ....

   b 1.2 g of carbon is added to another beaker.

     Calculate the number of atoms in this beaker.

     Write your answer in standard form.

     ....

     ....

3 A student measures a cuboid of aluminium.

$a = 2\,\text{cm}$, $b = 2\,\text{cm}$, $c = 5\,\text{cm}$

   a Write each length in metres.

     ....

     ....

     ....

   b **i** Calculate the volume of the cube ($a \times b \times c$).

        ....

     ii Write the volume in standard form.

        ....

   The mass of the cube was measured as 0.054 kg.

   c **i** Calculate the density of the cube $\left(\dfrac{\text{mass}}{\text{volume}}\right)$.

        ....

        ....

     ii Write the density rounded to one significant figure.

        ....

Working with data

Why do you need to work with data in chemistry?

Our understanding of chemistry has been developed through the observation of the world around us. Two types of data may be collected. In chemistry:

- **qualitative data** are often a description of an observation, such as a colour change
- **quantitative data** are based on numbers that have been obtained by measurement.

Data measured on a scale are **continuous data**, but the value of any particular measurement is always an approximation. Measurements always have a level of **uncertainty**.

Maths focus 1: Collecting data

You can gather data in different ways. Think about a simple experiment in which marble chips are added to hydrochloric acid (see Figure 2.1).

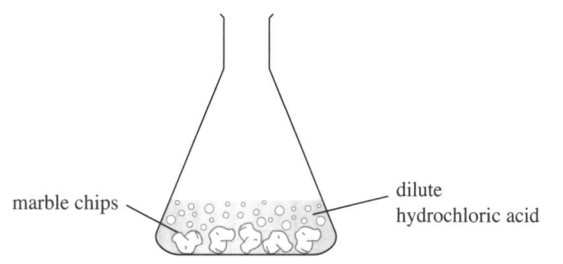

Figure 2.1 The reaction of marble chips with dilute hydrochloric acid

You could make careful observations to create a *qualitative* description of the reaction.

Quantitative data give you more information about the reaction. For example, you could measure the volume of gas produced every 30 seconds (see Figure 2.2). This numerical data can be plotted on a graph and used to find patterns and **trends** in how fast the reaction takes place.

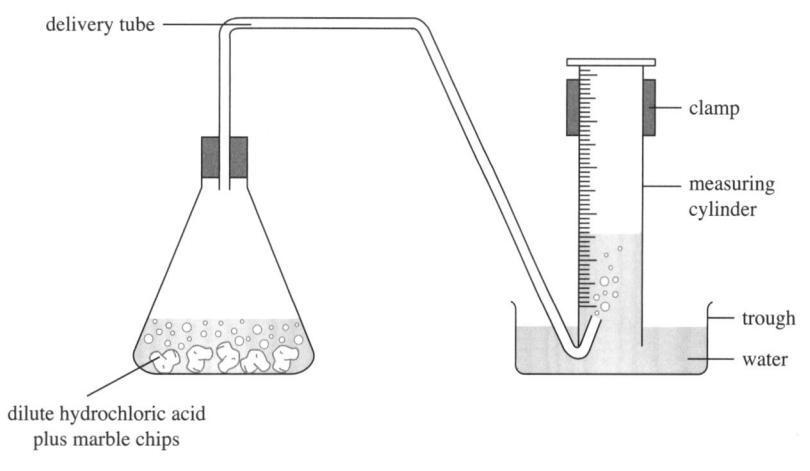

Figure 2.2 Measuring the amount of gas produced

What maths skills do you need to collect data?

1	Reading scales	• Find the level of the liquid
		• Read the largest number before this level on the scale
		• Count the small divisions between this and the level of liquid
		• Add the volume shown by the number of small divisions to the larger number on the scale
2	Recording to the correct number of decimal places	• Write down the reading of the scale division that is exactly at, or just before, the level when reading from small to large on the scale
		• Decide whether the level is nearer the marked scale division or the half-way point between divisions and record the number appropriately

Maths skills practice

How does collecting data help to understand reactions?

- *Digital* measuring equipment, such as a balance, pH meter or temperature probe, displays the measurement directly. The measurements can give you information about a reaction at the beginning and at the end, and even how the quantities change during a reaction.
- *Non-digital* equipment, such as a thermometer, uses a **scale**. A scale is made up of equally spaced divisions with numbers marked at regular intervals. These numbers usually increase in 1s, 2s, 5s or 10s.

The number of decimal places that you use when recording a measurement is important because it gives information about the level of uncertainty of a measurement. For example, a temperature recorded with no decimal places (such as 24 °C) indicates greater uncertainty than a temperature recorded to one decimal place (such as 24.5 °C).

It is essential that you can read a scale carefully so that you are not adding to the uncertainty of the measurement.

Chapter 2: Working with data

Maths skill 1: Reading scales

WORKED EXAMPLE 1

The diagram shows part of a 10 cm³ measuring cylinder. What volume of liquid is shown on the scale?

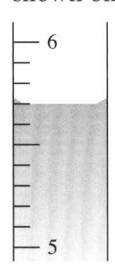

Step 1 Find the level of the liquid.

When reading a volume scale, you should always take the measurement from the bottom of the meniscus, making sure that the surface of the water is at your eye level.

Step 2 Read the *largest* number before this level on the scale.

The largest number on the scale, below the meniscus, is 5.

Step 3 Count the small divisions above this, to the level of liquid.

The meniscus of the liquid is 7 small divisions above 5.

Step 4 Add the volume shown by the number of small divisions to the larger number on the scale.

Work out what each division represents.

There are ten small divisions between 5 and 6 so each division is equal to 0.1 cm³.

The meniscus of the liquid is 7 small divisions above the 5, so the total volume of liquid is: 5 + (7 × 0.1) = 5.7

Don't forget to give the correct units.

The volume is 5.7 cm³.

> **TIP**
> The surface of water is curved. This is called the **meniscus**.

Practice question 1

What temperature is shown on each thermometer? (All the thermometers are marked in degrees Celsius, °C,)

a ....

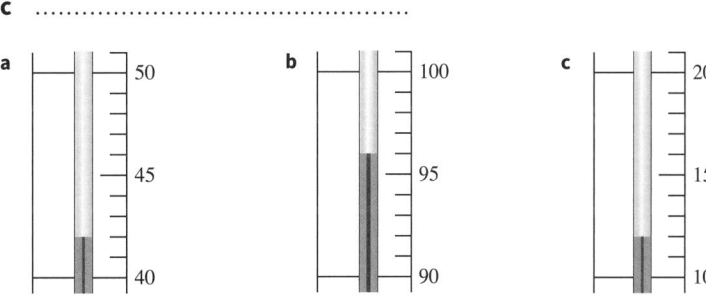

b ....

c ....

Cambridge IGCSE Chemistry Maths Skills

> **WATCH OUT**
> The scales on the measuring cylinders are different.

Practice question 2

What volume of liquid is there in each measuring cylinder?

(All the measuring cylinders are marked in cubic centimetres, cm³.)

a ....

b ....

c ....

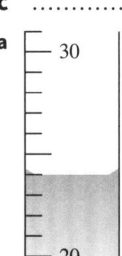

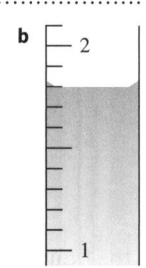

> **WATCH OUT**
> The scale on a burette is numbered from top to bottom, so the larger numbers are at the bottom of the scale. You must read it in the opposite direction from a measuring cylinder.

Practice question 3

What volume of liquid is shown in each burette? (Both burettes are marked in cubic centimetres, cm³)

a ....

b ....

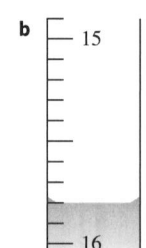

Maths skill 2: Recording to the correct number of decimal places

The more accurate a measurement is, the closer it is to the true value. Using a measuring instrument with greater **resolution** helps to improve **accuracy**. There is less uncertainty in measurements taken with an instrument with better resolution.

The resolution of most thermometers is actually the value of half a division, because this is the smallest change that can be measured. For a thermometer with divisions marked every 1 °C, the resolution is 0.5 °C.

You should therefore record measurements from a thermometer correct to one decimal place (for example, 24.0 °C not 24 °C). This shows that there is less uncertainty in the measurement than simply recording the temperature to the nearest whole number (no decimal places).

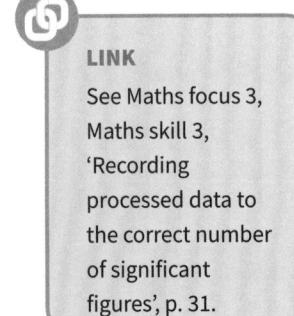

> **LINK**
> See Maths focus 3, Maths skill 3, 'Recording processed data to the correct number of significant figures', p. 31.

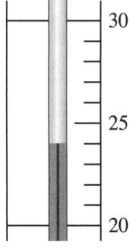

Chapter 2: Working with data

On a burette the smallest divisions represent 0.1 cm³.

Burettes can also be read to the nearest half division (0.05 cm³).

The readings from a burette should be recorded to two decimal places.

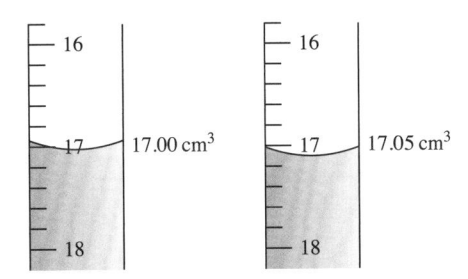

17.00 cm³   17.05 cm³

WORKED EXAMPLE 2

Record the thermometer reading to the correct number of decimal places.

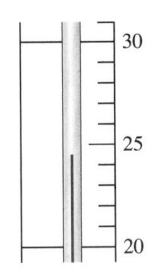

Step 1 Write down the reading of the scale division that is exactly at, or just before, the level when reading from small to large on the scale.

KEY QUESTIONS TO ASK YOURSELF:

- Does the scale read from top to bottom, or bottom to top, of the measuring instrument?

  In this case the scale reads from bottom to top. The numbers increase going up the thermometer.

  On a burette the scale reads from top to bottom. The numbers increase going down the burette.

- Is the scale division just below or just above the level of the liquid?

  In this case you need to read the division that is exactly at or just below the level, 24.

  On a burette you need to read the division that is exactly at or just above the level of the liquid.

Step 2 Decide whether the level is nearer the marked scale division or the half-way point between divisions and record the number appropriately.

This reading is nearer the half-way point.

This reading should be written:

24.5 °C

WATCH OUT

If the reading level is nearer the marked division, write 0 at the end of the number. Remember to add a decimal point if necessary.

If the level is nearer the half-way point between divisions, write 5 at the end of the number. Remember to add a decimal point if necessary.

TIP

Always remember to give the correct units.

Cambridge IGCSE Chemistry Maths Skills

Practice question 4

Write down the temperature shown on each thermometer, to the correct number of decimal places.

a ....

b ....

c ....

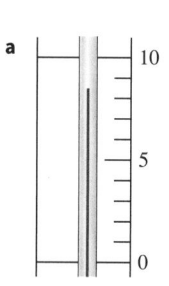

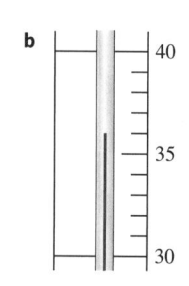

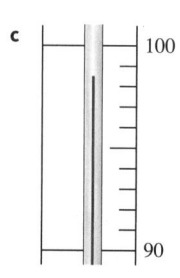

Practice question 5

Write down the volume shown on each burette, to the correct number of decimal places.

a ....

b ....

c ....

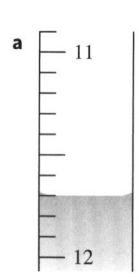

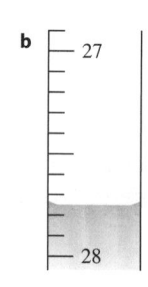

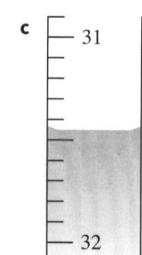

Maths focus 2: Understanding types of data

The design of an experiment influences the type of data produced. Usually there will be one **independent variable** that is changed each time, and one **dependent variable** that is measured each time the independent variable is changed.

Often, these variables are numerical (the measurements will be written as numbers). Usually the variable can take on any value, such as when measuring length, temperature or mass. This is known as continuous data.

On other occasions, measurements are made for a range of different categories, for example, types of material. The independent variable that is being changed each time in this case is the type of material. This is not a number and is known as **categorical data**.

Sometimes an independent variable can only take on certain values. In this case it is known as **discrete data**. This type of data is less common in chemistry.

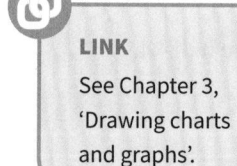

LINK

See Chapter 3, 'Drawing charts and graphs'.

Chapter 2: Working with data

> **LINK**
> See Chapter 3, Maths Focus 3, 'Drawing line graphs'.

What maths skills do you need to understand different types of data?

1	Identifying the independent and dependent variables	• Identify the variable that was changed during the experiment (the independent variable)
		• Identify the variable that was measured each time (the dependent variable)
2	Distinguishing categorical, continuous and discrete data	• Decide whether the independent variable is recorded as words or numbers
		• Decide whether numerical data can take on any value

> **WATCH OUT**
> For quantitative data, the dependent variable will always be numerical (either continuous or discrete) but the independent variable may not be.

Maths skills practice

How does understanding different types of data help to decide what type of graph to draw?

There are different types of data:

- Some data can be sorted into categories (groups) but the categories cannot be easily ordered, for example, the names of materials. This is known as *categorical* data.
- Sometimes the numerical data can take any value within a certain **range**, for example, the temperature of an object. This is *continuous* data.
- *Discrete* data occur where the data can only take certain values, for example, the numbers of protons in an atom can only be whole numbers.

If the independent variable is categorical, present it on a **bar chart**. Label the categories of the independent variable along the horizontal **axis**.

> **LINK**
> See Chapter 3, Maths focus 1, 'Drawing bar charts'.

Always represent continuous data in a **line graph**, because the points between the plotted data also have values.

The independent variable should always be plotted on the horizontal axis, and the dependent variable on the vertical axis.

Maths skill 1: Identifying the independent and dependent variables

> **TIP**
> If a measurement is made at regular time intervals, then the independent variable is time.

WORKED EXAMPLE 3

Read the experiment description below. Write down the independent variable and the dependent variable.

A student adds some marble chips to hydrochloric acid and measures the temperature every 30 seconds for 5 minutes.

Step 1 Identify the variable that is changed each time (independent variable).

The student measures the temperature every 30 seconds, so the independent variable is time.

Step 2 Identify the variable that is measured each time the independent variable is changed (the dependent variable).

The student measures the temperature every 30 seconds, so the dependent variable is temperature.

> **TIP**
> The independent variable does not have to be a number. It could be the type of metal.

Cambridge IGCSE Chemistry Maths Skills

> **TIP**
> Sometimes a description of an experiment gives the units but not the name of the variable. You need to remember that measuring in cubic centimetres (cm^3) means that the variable is *volume* or that measuring in grams (g) means that the variable is *mass*.

Practice question 6

A student carries out four different experiments. Read the experiment description and write down the independent and dependent variables for each.

a A student adds $10\,cm^3$ of acid, $1\,cm^3$ at a time, to a beaker containing an alkali. She uses a pH meter to measure the pH each time.

....
....

b She then carries out another experiment and adds some marble chips to a flask containing acid. She measures the mass every 30 seconds for 5 minutes.

....
....

c For her third experiment the student adds sodium thiosulfate to hydrochloric acid and times how long it takes for the solution to turn cloudy. She repeats this at four different temperatures.

....
....

d Finally the student uses pH paper to test five different types of substance.

....
....

Practice question 7

A scientist finds the temperatures at which elements with different atomic numbers melt. In this experiment what is:

a the independent variable   **b** the dependent variable?

....

Maths skill 2: Distinguishing categorical, continuous and discrete data

WORKED EXAMPLE 4

Read the experiment description below. Write down whether the independent variable is categorical, continuous or discrete.

A student adds some marble chips to hydrochloric acid and measures the temperature every 30 seconds for 5 minutes.

Step 1 Decide whether the independent variable is recorded as words or numbers.

If it is recorded in words, then the data are categorical.

In this case the data are numerical so a further decision needs to be made.

Step 2 Decide whether the numerical data can take on any value.

The independent variable is time. This is recorded in numerals and can take on any value. This is because, even though the student has chosen to measure every 30 seconds, the values in between have meaning.

The independent variable is therefore continuous.

(If numerical data cannot take on any value they are discrete data.)

Chapter 2: Working with data

Practice question 8

Read the experiment descriptions in Practice questions 6 and 7 again. Write down whether each independent variable is categorical, continuous or discrete.

....

....

Maths focus 3: Recording and processing data

Data alone cannot help you to understand chemistry. Recording data helps to communicate measurements clearly to other people. It also helps you to process the data, for example, using maths to calculate the **mean** and other quantities.

Recording data clearly in a table makes it easier to plot a graph, and this helps you to identify any patterns or trends in the data.

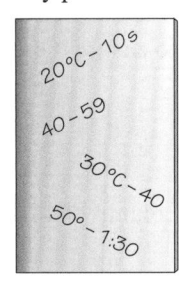

20°C – 10s
40 – 59
30°C – 40
50° – 1:30

Figure 2.3 Unorganised data

Figure 2.3 shows data recorded in an unorganised way. The units are not used consistently and the measurements are not presented in order.

Temperature °C	Time s
20	10
30	40
40	59
50	90

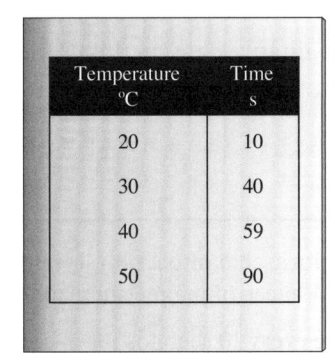

Figure 2.4 Organised data

Figure 2.4 shows the data recorded in a table. The units are the same throughout and the measurements are presented in a systematic way. This makes it easy to see a pattern in the data. As the temperature increases, the time increases.

What maths skills do you need to record and process data?

1	Drawing tables	• Work out how many columns and rows you need
		• Draw up the table
		• Add a heading to each column
		• Add the values of the independent variable
2	Drawing tables to help process data	• Work out how many extra columns you need
		• Draw the table, as described in Maths skill 1

Cambridge IGCSE Chemistry Maths Skills

3	Recording processed data to an appropriate number of significant figures	• Use a calculator to complete any calculations • Note the smallest number of significant figures that occurs in the data • Round the calculated values to this number of significant figures

Maths skills practice

How does recording and processing data help understand chemistry?

Drawing up a clear table helps to present information about different substances so that their properties can be compared.

Using a table also helps to organise data, making it easier to plot a graph, which in turn makes it easier to identify patterns and trends.

Processing data to work out the mean helps you to ensure there is less uncertainty in the data.

Maths skill 1: Drawing tables

Record the independent variable in the left-hand column of a table and the dependent variable in the right-hand column.

For categorical data, add words to the table in the left-hand column and add any numerical data for the dependent variable in the right-hand column.

For continuous and discrete data the independent variable is numerical. The values can be written in the left-hand column before the experiment begins.

You can also use a table to record qualitative data. In this case, record your observations in the right-hand column.

WORKED EXAMPLE 5

A student pours 20 ml of hydrochloric acid into a polystyrene cup and measures its temperature. She then adds a small piece of magnesium ribbon.

The student takes the temperature every 10 seconds for one minute.

Draw a table to record her data.

Step 1 Work out how many columns and how many rows she needs in her results table.

She needs two columns, one for the independent variable and one for the dependent variable.

The student measures the temperature at 0, 10, 20, 30, 40, 50 and 60 seconds (1 minute), so she needs a header row plus 7 more rows in the table.

Step 2 Draw up the table.

Step 3 Add the headings to each column.

The independent variable is time, with its unit s (for seconds), so the left-hand column heading is 'Time/s'.

The dependent variable is temperature, with its unit °C (for degrees Celsius), so the right-hand column heading is 'Temperature/°C'.

WATCH OUT
Always remember to separate the name of the variable and its unit symbol with a /. This can be called a slash, slant, solidus or stroke.

TIP
Adding the unit symbol to the column headings means that you don't have to write it after each number.

TIP
pH has no units because the pH scale is logarithmic, and this is beyond the requirements of this book.

Step 4 Add the values of the independent variable to the left-hand column.

The values of the independent variable are written out before the experiment starts.

Time s	Temperature °C
0	
10	
20	
30	
40	
50	
60	

Practice question 9

Draw a table to record the data for each experiment.

a A student adds 6 cm³ of acid, 1 cm³ at a time, to a beaker containing an alkali. He uses a pH meter to measure the pH each time.

b A student adds some marble chips to a flask containing acid. She measures the mass in grams (g) every 30 seconds for 3 minutes.

c A student adds sodium thiosulfate to hydrochloric acid (10 °C) and times, in seconds, how long it takes for the solution to turn cloudy. She repeats this at 20 °C, 30 °C and 40 °C.

d A student uses pH paper to test five different types of substance, A–E.

Maths skill 2: Drawing tables to help process data

Sometimes you need to apply mathematical processing to the data you collect, for example:

- You may need to calculate the mean for each set of repeated data.
- You may have measured the mass and volume of different metals in order to calculate the density.

Recording both the **raw data** and **processed data** in a well-organised table can help to make calculations easier.

WORKED EXAMPLE 6

A student times how long it takes 0.5 g of small marble chips to react with 25 cm^3 of acid. He repeats the experiment two more times until he has a set of three measurements.

He then carries out three similar experiments with medium marble chips, and another three experiments with large marble chips.

Draw up the table that he could use to record these results and calculate the mean.

Step 1 Work out how many columns are needed.

The student needs one column for the independent variable (size of marble chip) plus three columns for the dependent variable (time in seconds), because he needs to include the results of the three experiments for each chip size. He also needs an extra column to record the mean that he calculates.

So, in total the student needs five columns in his table.

Step 2 Draw the table, as described in Maths skill 1.

Work out how many rows the student needs.

The student is testing three sizes of marble chip so after the header row he needs three more rows.

Add the heading to each column.

The independent variable is the size of the marble chips. This does not have a unit.

There are three columns for the dependent variable (Time/s). This needs one overall heading above and three separate column headings: Test 1, Test 2, Test 3 below.

Time s		
Test 1	Test 2	Test 3

The column on the right of the table should have the heading 'Mean', with the correct unit symbol (the same as the dependent variable) of s for seconds.

Add the values of the independent variable that are going to be tested to the left-hand column. In this case the independent variable is categorical, so the words 'small', 'medium' and 'large' need to be added.

Size of marble chip	Time s			Mean/s
	Test 1	Test 2	Test 3	
small				
medium				
large				

Practice question 10

Draw up the table for each student's experiment described below.

a A student adds sodium thiosulfate solution to hydrochloric acid at 20 °C and measures the time it takes for the solution to turn cloudy. He carries out the experiment two more times. He then carries out the experiment three times at 30 °C and three times at 40 °C.

b Another student is finding out the density of four pieces of metal (copper, iron aluminium and tin). She finds the volume and mass of each piece of metal and records these in a table. She then works out the density, using the **formula**:

$$\text{density} = \frac{\text{mass}}{\text{volume}}$$

> **TIP**
> The order of columns can help with calculations. Put the columns in the order that the numbers will be used in the calculation.

Maths skill 3: Recording processed data to the correct number of significant figures

When you carry out a calculation with experimental data, the number of significant figures in your answer should be the same as the smallest number of significant figures used in the data values. Your calculated answer should not seem to show more accuracy than occurs in the original measurements.

However, there are other factors that can result in uncertainty. **Random errors** often occur when you are carrying out an experiment. Working out the mean of repeated measurements reduces uncertainty due to random errors.

Repeat results that are close together indicate that the data are **precise**. However, even if results are in close agreement this does not necessarily mean that the data values are accurate. There could be a **systematic error** that is making all the data slightly too large or too small. An example of a systematic error could be a zeroing error on a balance.

> **LINK**
> See Chapter 1 for more on significant figures.

Chapter 2: Working with data

LINK

See Chapter 1, Maths focus 3, Maths skill 2, 'Writing numbers to the correct number of significant figures (sf)'.

WATCH OUT

If you have more than one set of measurements (for example, mass and volume), remember to use the number of significant figures in the data value that has the smallest number of significant figures.

TIP

A reading that is very different to the others it is called an **outlier**. If you can explain why the measurement is so different (for example, due to an error in the experiment) then it should be ignored when calculating the mean.

WORKED EXAMPLE 7

A student measures the volume of carbon dioxide produced during a reaction.

Calculate the mean volume of the three measurements. Record your answer to an appropriate number of significant figures.

Volume cm³		
Test 1	Test 2	Test 3
22.4	22.2	21.8

Step 1 Use a calculator to complete any calculations.

Calculate the mean:

$$\frac{22.4 + 22.2 + 21.8}{3} = 22.1333$$

Step 2 Note the lowest number of significant figures in the data.

Each measurement has three significant figures.

Step 3 Round the calculated values to this number of significant figures.

22.1 cm³

Practice question 11

a A student used a burette to measure the volume of acid required to neutralise an alkali. She carried out the experiment three times. Calculate the mean result of the three experiments. Record the mean to an appropriate number of significant figures.

Volume cm³		
Test 1	Test 2	Test 3
20.05	20.10	19.95

....

b A student times how long it takes for a reaction to form 20 cm³ of hydrogen gas.

It takes 16 seconds.

Calculate the mean rate of reaction: $\frac{\text{volume}}{\text{time}}$

....

c A student measured how much the mass decreased during a reaction. The reaction took 10 s. The loss of mass was 1.24 g. Calculate the mean rate of reaction: $\frac{\text{mass}}{\text{time}}$

....

Further questions

1 A student investigated the density of three lumps of metal.

First she used a balance to find the mass of each lump of metal.

Then she added 5.0 cm³ of water to a measuring cylinder. She then dropped a lump of iron into the measuring cylinder and noted the new volume.

The change in volume was equal to the volume of the lump iron.

She recorded the mass and new volume in a table. She then calculated the volume of each lump and the density of each.

a Draw up a table for the student to record her measurements and calculations.

The measuring cylinder and digital balance readings are shown below. Record the measurements in the table.

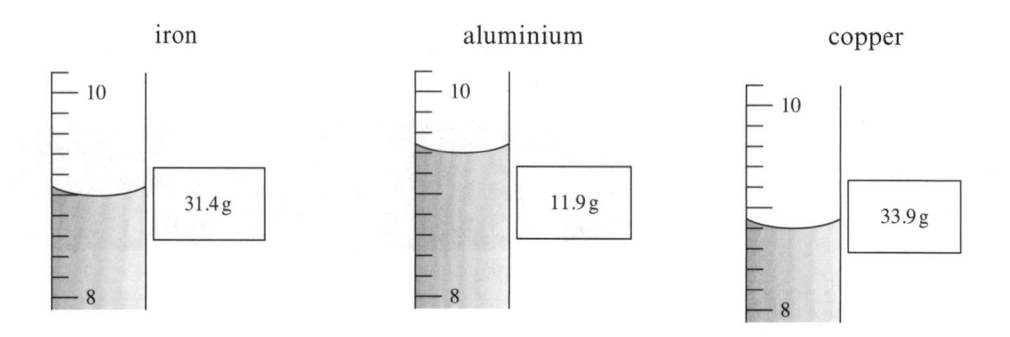

iron — 31.4 g

aluminium — 11.9 g

copper — 33.9 g

b Calculate the density of each metal and record in the table to an appropriate number of significant figures.

....
....
....

2 The temperature was measured during two different reactions. Each experiment was carried out three times.

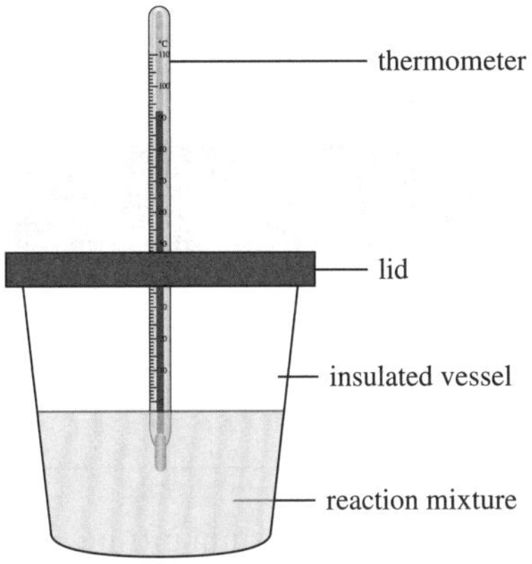

Reaction 1: Copper sulfate solution + zinc powder

a Record the maximum temperature measurements in the table below.

Experiment	Thermometer diagram	Maximum temperature of solution °C	Temperature change °C
1	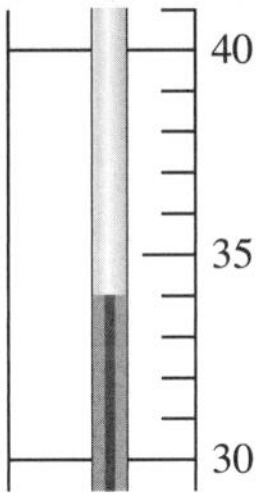		
2	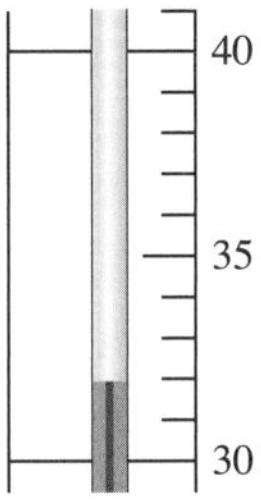		
3	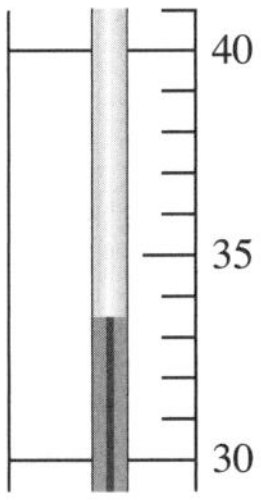		

b The temperature of the solution was 23 °C at the start. Calculate the temperature change for each experiment and record this in the table.

c Calculate the mean change for the copper sulfate + zinc reaction, giving your answer to an appropriate number of significant figures.

....

Reaction 2: Potassium nitrate + water

Test	Maximum temperature of solution °C	Temperature change °C
1	20.5	−2.5
2	20.0	−3.0
3	19.0	−4.0

d Calculate the mean change for the potassium nitrate + water reaction to an appropriate number of significant figures.

....

....

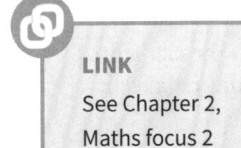

Drawing charts and graphs

Why do you need to draw charts and graphs in chemistry?

Using charts and graphs makes it easier to compare data values and to look for patterns. This sort of visual display is less useful if you want to share the actual values. A table is better for this.

Types of graph used in chemistry

You can use different types of graph or chart to represent data. The most common types that you are likely to need in chemistry are:
- bar charts
- pie charts
- line graphs.

> **LINK**
> See Chapter 2, Maths focus 2 'Understanding types of data'.

Maths focus 1: Drawing bar charts

A bar chart is useful for comparing categorical data. If the independent variable is not numerical you should always use a bar chart. Discrete data are also usually shown on a bar chart.

For example, the bar chart shown in Figure 3.1 makes it easy to compare the main uses of water in a UK home.

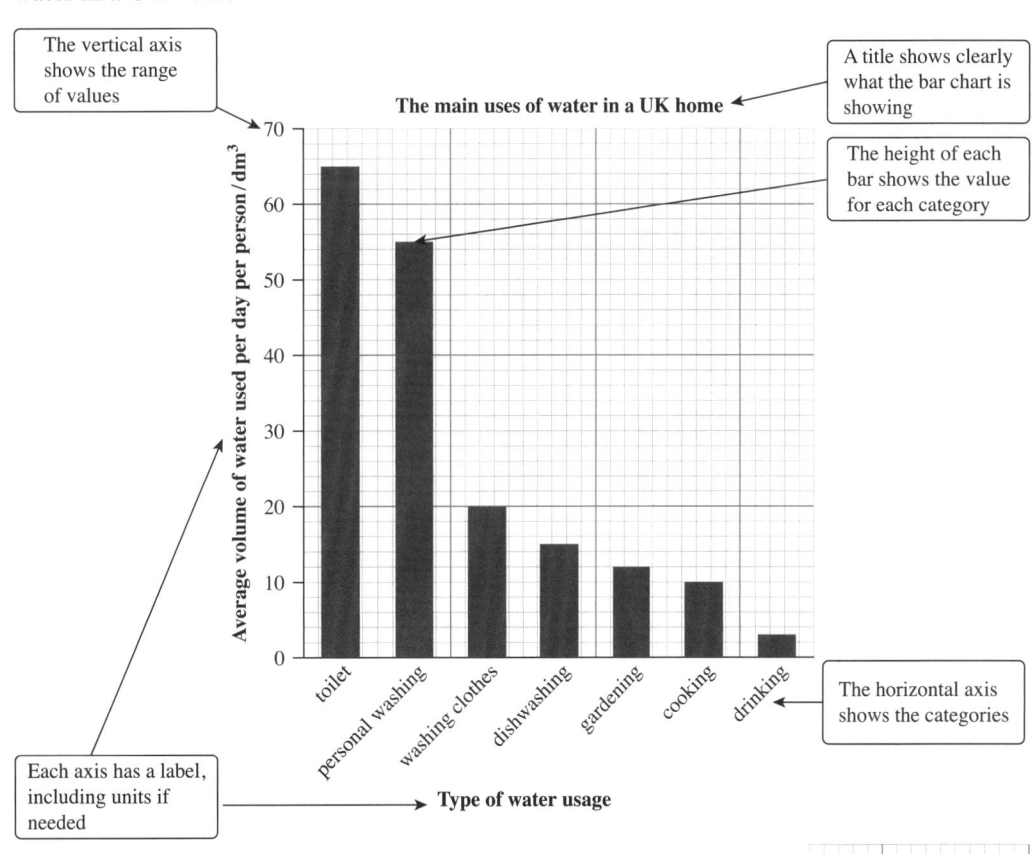

> **TIP**
> In algebraic graphs showing a relation between two variables, x and y, the horizontal axis is generally the x-axis and the vertical axis is generally the y-axis. It is common practice to use these terms to describe the axes in any graph. In this case, the horizontal axis shows types of water usage and the vertical axis shows the volume of water used.

Annotations on Figure 3.1:
- The vertical axis shows the range of values
- A title shows clearly what the bar chart is showing
- The height of each bar shows the value for each category
- The horizontal axis shows the categories
- Each axis has a label, including units if needed

Figure 3.1 The features of a bar chart

The graph paper you will use most often will be made up of large, medium and small squares, as shown in Figure 3.2.

Each large square is divided into four medium-sized squares, and each of these medium squares comprises a grid of 25 small squares.

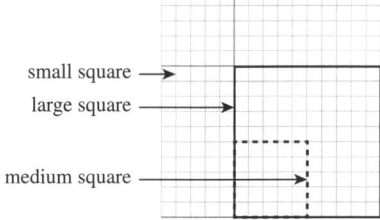

Figure 3.2 Typical graph paper

Cambridge IGCSE Chemistry Maths Skills

What maths skills do you need to draw a bar chart?

1	Choosing a suitable scale for the vertical axis	• Find the maximum value needed on the vertical axis • Choose a scale that is easy to read and takes up at least half of the available space
2	Drawing the bars	• Draw and label the axes • Use the vertical scale to work out the heights of the bars • Draw bars with the same width, leaving a small gap between them

Maths skills practice

How does drawing a bar chart help you understand patterns in the properties of the elements?

Each chemical element has different properties. You can look up data about the elements, such as melting point, boiling point or density. Drawing a bar chart of this data makes it easier to compare these properties and to see any trends or patterns.

Maths skill 1: Choosing a suitable scale for the vertical axis

> **TIP**
> Always round to the nearest whole number.

> **TIP**
> If you need to draw a bar graph to show negative values you must use the same scale for the positive and negative parts of the axis.

> **TIP**
> The scale on an axis tells you how much each square on the graph paper represents. It makes the values easier to read if the side of each large square represents a value of 1, 2, 5 or a multiple of ten of these (10, 20, 50 or 0.1, 0.2, 0.5).

WORKED EXAMPLE 1

Table 3.1 shows the densities of different metal elements (rounded to one decimal place).

Element	Density g/cm³
aluminium	2.7
copper	8.9
iron	7.9
gold	19.3

The data are to be shown on a bar chart.

Which scale should be used for the vertical axis?

Table 3.1 Densities of different metal elements

Assume the grid supplied for the bar chart has a height of 5 large squares.

Step 1 Find the maximum value needed on the vertical axis.

The largest density value is 19.3 g/cm³. Rounding this up to the nearest whole number gives a maximum value of 20 g/cm³ on the vertical axis.

Step 2 Choose a scale that is easy to read and takes up at least half the available space.

Scale: 1 large square =	Largest value that can be plotted	Do data values fit?	Does scale take up over half of the grid?
1 g/cm³	5 g/cm³	no	–
2 g/cm³	10 g/cm³	no	–
5 g/cm³	25 g/cm³	yes	yes

Therefore 1 large square ≡ 5 g/cm³ is a suitable scale.

You can use the symbol ≡ to mean 'represents'.

Chapter 3: Drawing charts and graphs

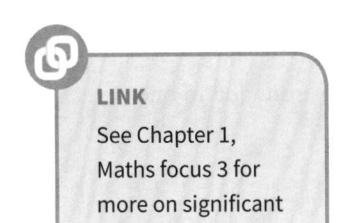

LINK

See Chapter 1, Maths focus 3 for more on significant figures.

Practice question 1

The data in Table 3.2 show the melting points of some Group 1 alkali metal elements, rounded to two significant figures.

Element	Melting point °C
sodium	98
potassium	64
rubidium	39
caesium	29

Table 3.2 Melting points of some Group 1 alkali metal elements

a Complete the table below to suggest three possible scales for a grid that has a height of 3 large squares.

Scale: 1 large square =	Largest value that can be plotted	Do data values fit?	Does scale take up over half of the grid?
2 °C			
20 °C			
40 °C			

b What is the best scale for the axis?

....

Practice question 2

The data in Table 3.3 show the melting points of some elements in the third period (row) of the Periodic Table, rounded to two significant figures.

Element	Melting point °C
sodium	98
magnesium	650
aluminium	660
silicon	1407

Table 3.3 Melting points of some elements in the third period of the Periodic Table

What is the best scale to use for the axis if the grid supplied has a height of 8 large squares?

1 large square ≡ .... °C

Cambridge IGCSE Chemistry Maths Skills

Maths skill 2: Drawing the bars

WORKED EXAMPLE 2

The data in Table 3.4 show the densities of three different elements, rounded to one decimal place. Draw a bar chart to compare these densities.

Element	Density g/cm³
aluminium	2.7
magnesium	1.7
lithium	0.5

Table 3.4 Densities of three different elements

Step 1 Draw and label the axes.

Remember that the categories (elements) go on the horizontal axis and the density is on the vertical axis.

The vertical axis should have a scale of 1 large square ≡ 1 g/cm³.

Step 2 Use the vertical scale to work out the heights of the bars.

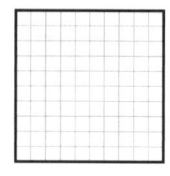

To work out the value of each small square, divide the value of a large square by 10 (the number of tiny squares along one side of a large square).

$$\frac{1}{10} \text{ g/cm}^3 = 0.1 \text{ g/cm}^3$$

Step 3 Draw the bars with the same width, leaving a small gap between them.

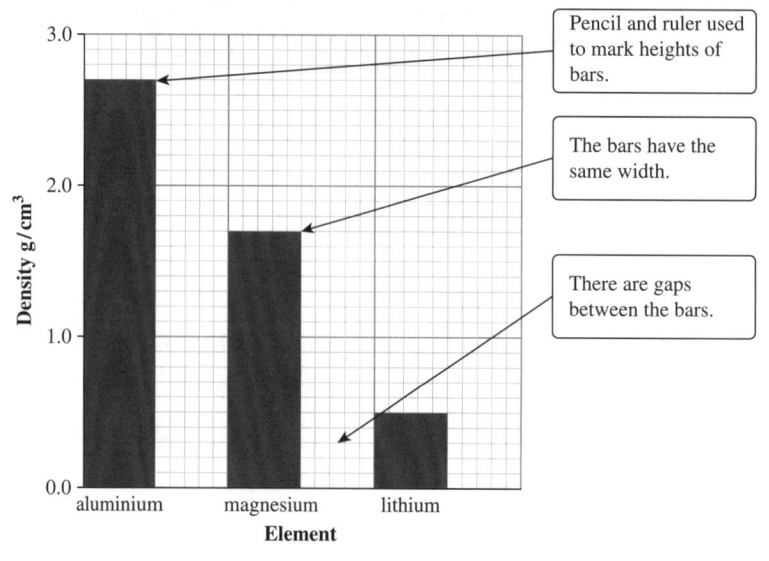

- Pencil and ruler used to mark heights of bars.
- The bars have the same width.
- There are gaps between the bars.

Figure 3.3 Densities of three different elements

Practice question 3

Draw a bar chart to compare the densities of three of the Group 1 alkali metals as shown in Table 3.5.

Element	Density g/cm³
lithium	0.53
sodium	0.97
potassium	0.86

Table 3.5 Densities of three Group 1 alkali metals

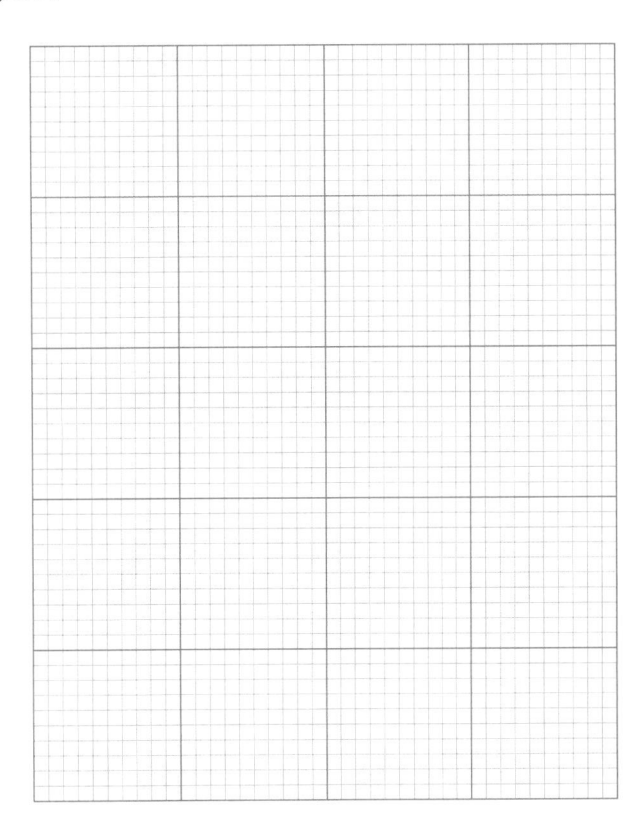

a Draw and label the axes on the grid below. The vertical axis should have a scale of 1 large square ≡ 0.2 g/cm³.

b What does each small square on this axis represent? ....

c Draw the three bars on your chart.

Practice question 4

Draw a bar chart to compare the boiling points of five noble gases, as shown in Table 3.6.

Element	Boiling point °C
neon	−246
argon	−186
krypton	−152
xenon	−108
radon	−62

Table 3.6 Boiling points of five noble gases

Cambridge IGCSE Chemistry Maths Skills

> **WATCH OUT**
> When the vertical axis includes negative values, it should extend below the horizontal axis.

a Draw and label the axes on the grid below. The vertical axis should have a scale of 1 large square ≡ 50 °C.

> **WATCH OUT**
> The larger the **magnitude** of the negative number, the further down the axis it should be plotted.

> **TIP**
> You may need to round your data values, depending upon the scale of your axis.

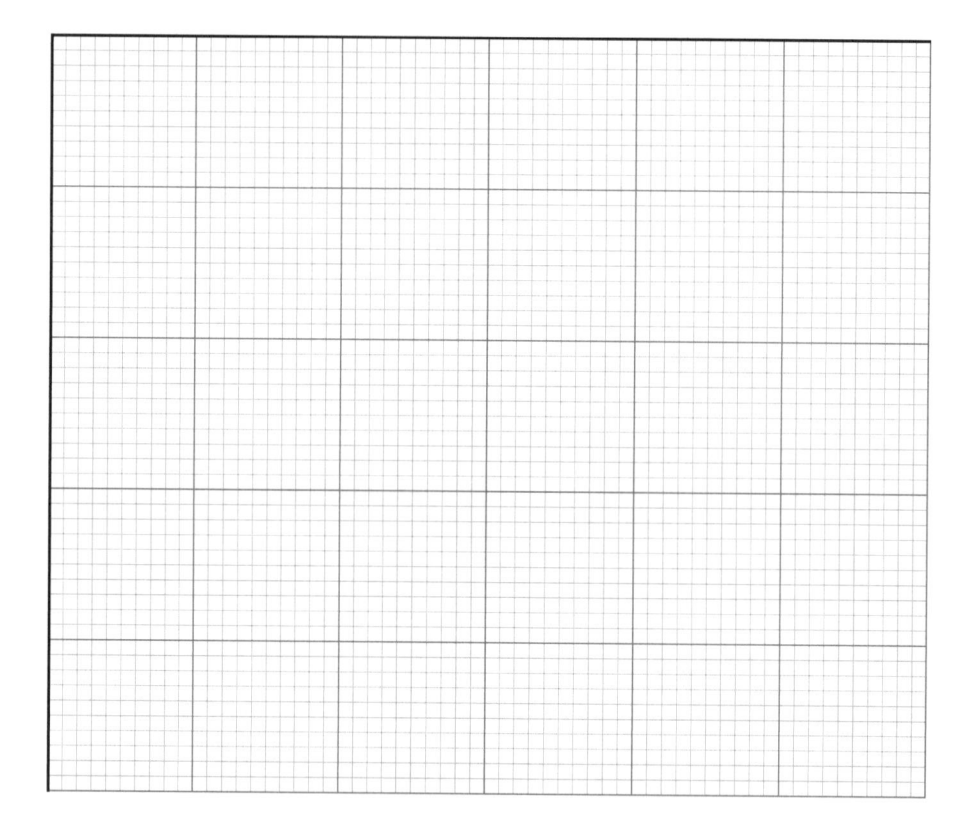

b What does each small square on the vertical axis represent?

....

c Draw the five bars on your chart.

Maths focus 2: Drawing pie charts

In chemistry, **pie charts** are less commonly used than bar charts. This is partly because they are not suitable for showing direct measurements of a dependent variable for different values of an independent variable.

However, a pie chart is useful when comparing proportions or **percentages** that make up a whole. Each of the separate categories within the data is represented by a sector of the circle.

For example, the pie chart in Figure 3.4 shows the percentages of different gases in the air. Note that it has been drawn with the largest component starting at the top and being measured clockwise. This is a useful convention to follow.

Chapter 3: Drawing charts and graphs

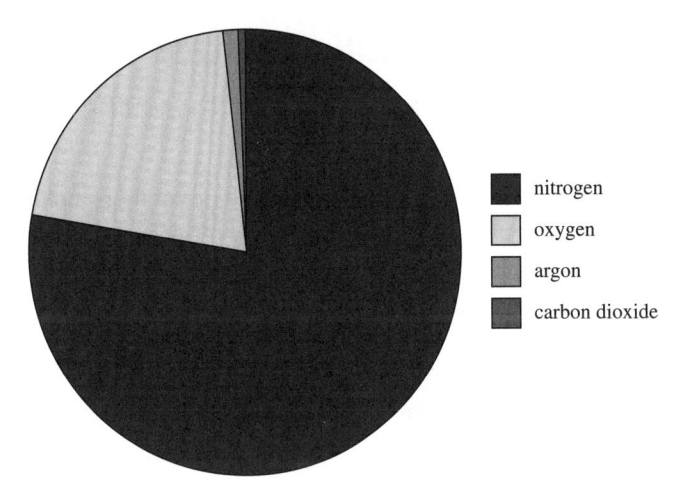

Figure 3.4 Percentages of different gases in the air

Not all percentage data can be shown in a pie chart. For example, the graph in Figure 3.5 shows the percentages of students who have used different types of transport to school during one week.

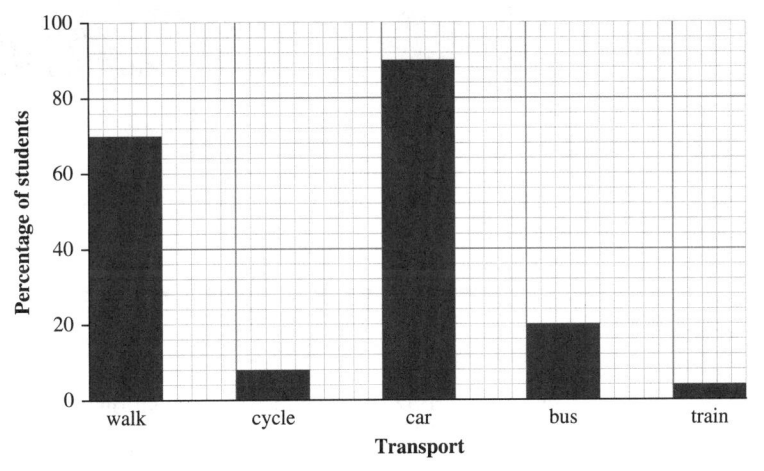

Figure 3.5 How students came to school last week

The percentages do not add up to 100 because some students may have used more than one type of transport during the week. The data were not all collected on one day but over a week so, for example, some students may have walked on some days and cycled on others. This type of percentage data cannot be presented in a pie chart.

The percentages of all the categories shown on a pie chart *must* add up to 100%.

What maths skills do you need to draw a pie chart?

1	Converting percentages to angles	• Multiply each percentage by 3.6° (see Tip for explanation) • Check that the angles add up to 360°
2	Drawing sectors	• List the percentages in order, from largest to smallest • Draw a circle with a vertical line (radius) upward from the centre • Use a protractor to measure and mark the first angle, then draw the first line • Move your protractor around so that it lies on this new line before measuring next angle (repeat)

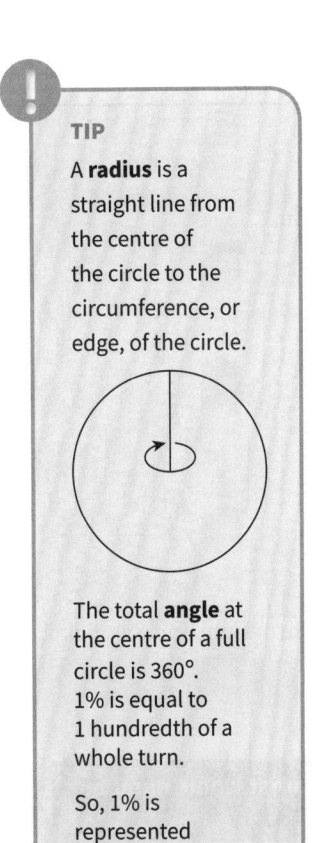

> **TIP**
> A **radius** is a straight line from the centre of the circle to the circumference, or edge, of the circle.
>
> The total **angle** at the centre of a full circle is 360°. 1% is equal to 1 hundredth of a whole turn.
>
> So, 1% is represented by $\frac{360°}{100} = 3.6°$.

Cambridge IGCSE Chemistry Maths Skills

Maths skills practice

How does drawing a pie chart help to understand the composition of different alloys?

An alloy is formed by mixing two or more molten metals, then allowing them to cool. The composition of this mixture is crucial in determining the properties of this mixture. The sectors on a pie chart give a clear visual comparison of the percentages of each metal in the alloy mixture.

Maths skill 1: Converting percentages to angles

> **TIP**
> Sometimes you may need to round the angles to the nearest whole degree. It is important to check that the angles still add up to 360 °C.

WORKED EXAMPLE 3

The alloy brass has a typical composition of 70% copper and 30% zinc.

What angles should each sector be on a pie chart to show this?

Step 1 Multiply each percentage by 3.6°.

× 3.6

Metal	Percentage %	Angle °
copper	70	252°
zinc	30	108°

Step 2 Check that the angles add up to 360°.

252° + 108° = 360°

> **WATCH OUT**
> Check the form of the data that you are given and remember to convert them into percentages if they are not already in that format. A pie chart shows a category as a percentage of the whole. Pie charts cannot be used to display data that have not been changed into percentages (or fractions).

Practice question 5

The alloy bronze has a typical composition of 90% copper and 10% tin.

What should the sector angles be on a pie chart to represent this?

Complete the table.

Metal	Percentage %	Angle °
copper	90	
tin	10	

Practice question 6

The alloy stainless steel has a typical composition of 74% iron, 18% chromium and 8% nickel.

What should each sector angle be on a pie chart to represent this?

Complete the table.

Metal	Percentage %	Angle °	Angle rounded to nearest whole number °
iron	74		
chromium	18		
nickel	8		
Total angle			360°

> **TIP**
> If you want to calculate the angles without using a calculator, remember that every 10% is represented by 36° in the pie chart. 50% is 180° and 25% is 90°.

Chapter 3: Drawing charts and graphs

Maths skill 2: Drawing sectors

WORKED EXAMPLE 4

Amalgum is an alloy that can be used in dental fillings. Its composition is shown in Table 3.7.

Metal	Percentage %	Angle °
mercury	50	180
silver	25	90
copper	10	36
tin	15	54

Table 3.7 Composition of amalgum

Draw a pie chart to show the composition of amalgum (with the sectors arranged in order of size).

Step 1 List the percentages in order, from largest to smallest.

  mercury   180°
  silver   90°
  tin   54°
  copper   36°

Step 2 Draw a circle plus a vertical line (radius) from the centre.

Mark a point at the top of the circle and draw the first line vertically from the centre to this point (the radius).

Step 3 Use a protractor to measure and mark the first angle, then draw the first line.

To do this, place your protractor so that the base line of the protractor (the line through 0/180 at both ends, and the centre) lies along the vertical line and the centre of the protractor is over the centre of the circle.

Measure and mark your first angle (180°). Be sure to choose the correct scale on the protractor.

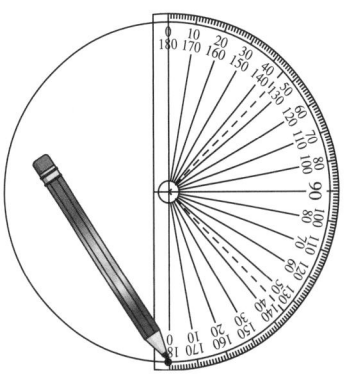

> **TIP**
> Make sure the angles add up to 360°.

Place your ruler so that it aligns with the centre of the circle and your angle mark and draw in the radius.

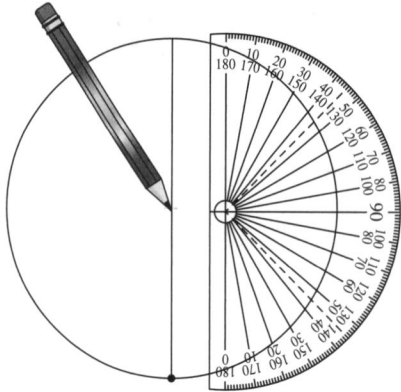

Step 4 Move your protractor around so the base line lies on this new line and the centre is over the centre of the circle before measuring the next angle.

Mark the angle and draw the radius to complete the second sector.

Move your protractor around so that it lies on this new line and line up the centre of the protractor with the centre of the circle.

Measure and mark your next angle and draw the radius. Repeat the previous process until you have drawn all the sectors.

As a check, measure the final angle to make sure it is correct (in this case 36°).

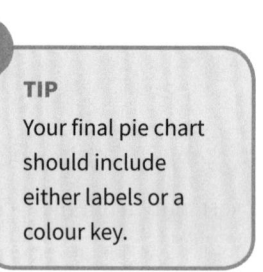

The composition of amalgum

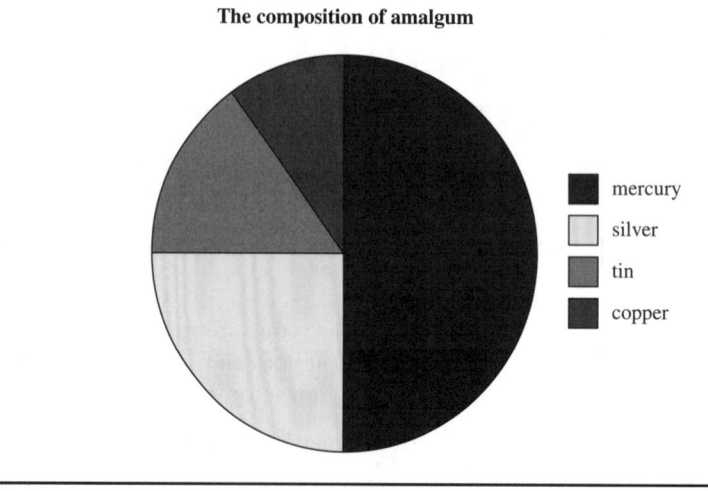

- mercury
- silver
- tin
- copper

TIP
Your final pie chart should include either labels or a colour key.

Practice question 7

White gold is an alloy. Its composition is shown in Table 3.8.

Metal	Percentage %	Angle °
gold	75	270
palladium	10	36
nickel	10	36
zinc	5	18

Table 3.8 Composition of white gold

Draw a pie chart to show the composition of white gold.

> **TIP**
> When the angle is greater than 180°, subtract it from 360° and measure anticlockwise.

Practice question 8

Solder used to be an alloy of tin with lead but modern solder has a different composition, as shown in Table 3.9.

Metal	Percentage %	Angle °
tin	90	324
silver	5	18
copper	5	18

Table 3.9 Composition of solder

Draw a pie chart to show the composition of solder.

Cambridge IGCSE Chemistry Maths Skills

Maths focus 3: Drawing line graphs

There are two types of line graph:

- a point-to-point line graph
- a best-fit line graph.

In a *point-to-point line graph*, the plotted points are all connected (point to point). In this type of graph you assume that each plotted point shows the actual values of the data at that moment. In chemistry, as for other graphs, the independent variable (generally time) is plotted on the horizontal axis and the dependent variable is plotted on the vertical axis. Readings are taken over a series of time intervals. There is often no **linear relationship** between the independent and dependent variables. The points do not lie in a straight line, they may even appear to go up and down. The lines between plotted points may not be used to read off values between them.

For example, the point-to-point line graph in Figure 3.6 shows levels of NO_x (nitrogen oxides) in a city recorded at 2-hourly intervals.

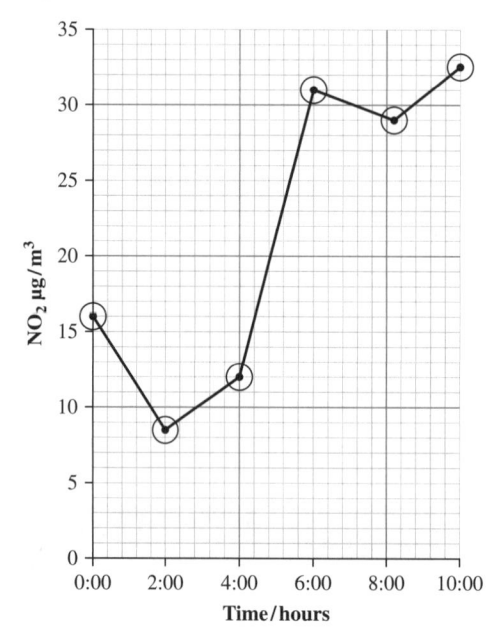

Figure 3.6 A point-to-point line graph showing levels of NO_x (nitrogen oxides) at different times in a city

In the second type of graph, the relationship between the dependent and independent variables is shown by a **best-fit line**.

It is assumed that the actual values lie on this line (or curve) even if the actual measured values do not, because of measurement errors.

In chemistry lines (or curves) of best fit are used to plot data relating to rates of reaction. This is the type of line graph that you will usually need to draw. However, you may see a point-to-point line graph used, for example, to show air pollution measurements at different times in a city as above.

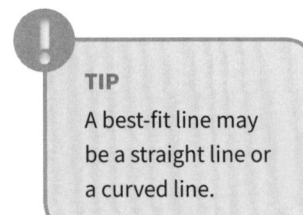

> **TIP**
> A best-fit line may be a straight line or a curved line.

Chapter 3: Drawing charts and graphs

This graph in Figure 3.7 shows how mass varies with volume for aluminium. The graph is drawn as a best-fit line because the measured values do not lie exactly on the line, due to uncertainties in the measurements. The best-fit line is closer to the true values.

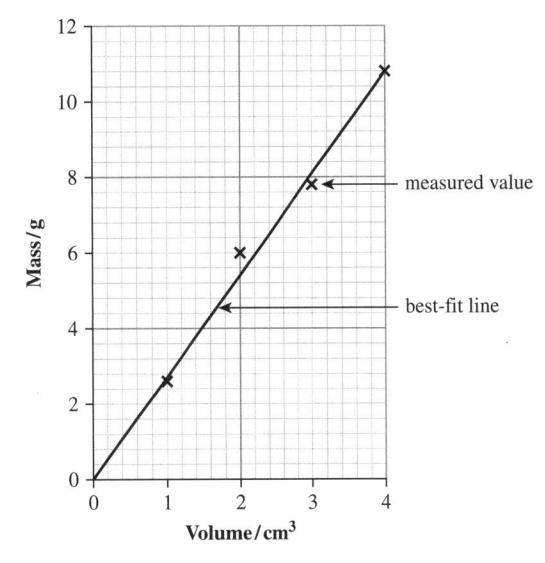

Figure 3.7 The relationship between mass and volume of aluminium

The graph in Figure 3.8 shows the volume of hydrogen produced every minute during a reaction between magnesium and hydrochloric acid. The points clearly form a curve but do not lie exactly on the curve. A *curved* line of best fit gives a better indication of the true values.

> **TIP**
> Always think about the chemistry behind the graph. This graph must have a curved line of best fit because there is a maximum volume of hydrogen that can be produced. A straight line of best fit would be incorrect.

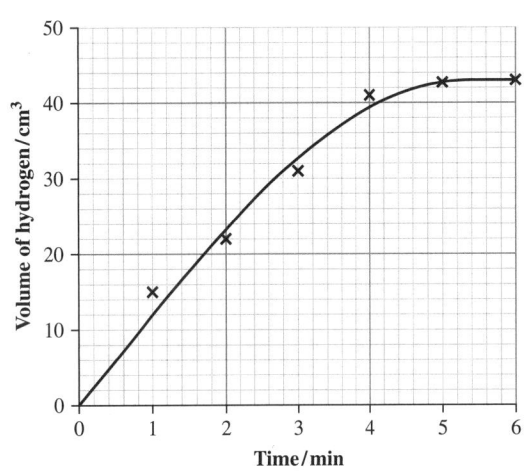

Figure 3.8 The volume of hydrogen produced over time during a reaction between magnesium and hydrochloric acid

> **LINK**
> Lines of best fit are discussed further in Chapter 4, Maths focus 2 'Reading values from a line graph'.

What maths skills do you need to draw a line graph?

1	Choosing which variable goes on which axis	• Identify the independent and dependent variables
		• Name the variable that goes on each axis
2	Drawing the axes	• Select an appropriate range and scale for each axis
		• Draw the axes and mark the scales
		• Label each axis with the correct variable and its units

3	Plotting the data points	• Find the values of a pair of measurements on the axes
		• Find the intersection and mark with a dot
		• Either draw a small circle around this dot or mark a small cross with the centre exactly over the dot
4	Using a ruler to draw a best-fit line	• Place a transparent ruler roughly in line with the points
		• Adjust the ruler to ensure a best-fit line
		• Draw the line carefully – use a sharp pencil
5	Drawing a best-fit curve freehand	• Picture the shape of the curve
		• Practise drawing the curve
		• Draw the curve using a sharp pencil

> **TIP**
>
> You can use **coordinate** notation to describe any point in terms of the values on the axes. The **origin**, where both values are zero, is written as (0, 0). The first number in the brackets gives the value along the horizontal axis, the second number gives the value up the vertical axis. If it helps, you can remember this as 'along the corridor and up the stairs'.

Maths skills practice

How does drawing a line graph help to interpret experimental data?

A line graph is a good way to examine the relationship between the independent and dependent variables. For example, a straight line of best fit through the point where the axes cross and both values are zero shows that the dependent variable is **directly proportional** to the independent variable. A curved line of best fit might show when a reaction stops and no more product is made. You can find out more about what the shape of a graph tells you in Chapter 4.

Maths skill 1: Choosing which variable goes on which axis

WORKED EXAMPLE 5

A student measures the masses of different volumes of aluminium.

Which variable should be shown on which axis?

Step 1 Identify the independent and dependent variables.

> **KEY QUESTIONS TO ASK YOURSELF:**
>
> • Which variable is changed each time?
>   The volume is changed each time, so this is the independent variable.
> • Which variable is measured each time?
>   The mass is measured each time, so this is the dependent variable.

Step 2 Name the variable that goes on each axis.

The independent variable (volume) goes on the horizontal axis.

The dependent variable (mass) does on the vertical axis.

Chapter 3: Drawing charts and graphs

LINK

A method for choosing a scale was explained in Maths Focus 1 'Drawing bar charts', Maths skill 1: 'Choosing a suitable scale for the vertical axis'.

Practice question 9

A student measures the volume of hydrogen produced every minute during a reaction.

Which variable should be shown on which axis?

.... should be on the horizontal axis.

.... should be on the vertical axis.

Practice question 10

A student reacts hydrochloric acid with sodium thiosulfate and times how long it takes for the resulting solution to turn cloudy. She then repeats the experiment with different concentrations of hydrochloric acid.

Which variable should be shown on which axis?

.... should be on the horizontal axis.

.... should be on the vertical axis.

Maths skill 2: Drawing the axes

TIP

The scale of an axis tells you how much each square on the graph paper represents. The values are easier to read if each large square has a value of 1, 2, 5 or a multiple of ten of these (10, 20, 50 or 0.1, 0.2, 0.5).

TIP

Each axis should take up over half the size of the grid you have available.

TIP

As the independent variable was measured every 1 cm³ it is sensible to mark every medium square.

WORKED EXAMPLE 6

A student measures the mass of different volumes of copper. This is her results table.

Volume cm³	Mass g
0	0
1	9
2	21
3	30
4	35

Draw suitable axes for a line graph to show these data values.

Assume that the grid provided is 2 large squares wide and 4 large squares in height.

Step 1 Select an appropriate range and scale for each axis.

The horizontal axis needs to take a range from 0 to 4 cm³ so a scale of 1 large square ≡ 2 cm³ would fit this range.

A range of 0 g to 40 g would fit on the vertical axis where each large square represents 10 g.

49

Cambridge IGCSE Chemistry Maths Skills

Scale: 1 large square ≡	Largest value that can be plotted*	Do data values fit?	Does scale take up over half of the grid?
5 g	20 g	No	
10 g	40 g	Yes	Yes

> **TIP**
> Avoid scales that make the values hard to plot or read.

Step 2 Draw the axes and mark the scales.

Draw the axes at right angles to each other, crossing at the origin, and of the right length to fit in the range of data.

Mark the scale with small, neat lines (called pecks or ticks) and number them.

Step 3 Label each axis with the correct variable and its units.

Write the labels in the form variable/units.

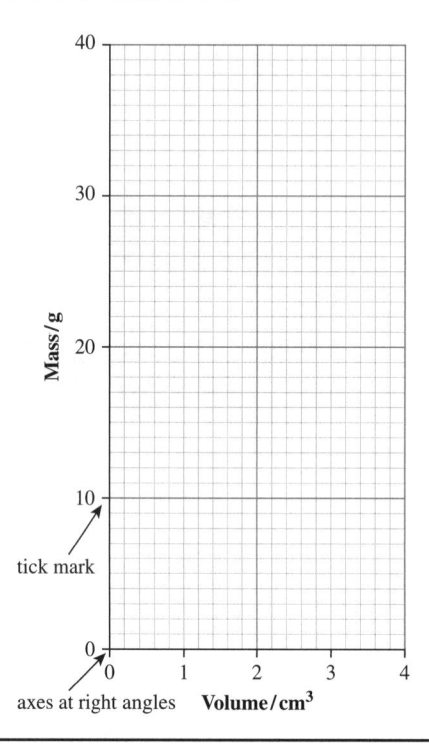

Practice question 11

The masses of different volumes of caesium are shown in Table 3.10.

Volume cm³	Mass g
0	0
1	1.9
2	3.8
3	5.7
4	7.6

Table 3.10 Masses of different volumes of caesium

Draw suitable axes for a line graph to show these data values.

Assume that the grid provided is 2 large squares wide and 8 large squares in height.

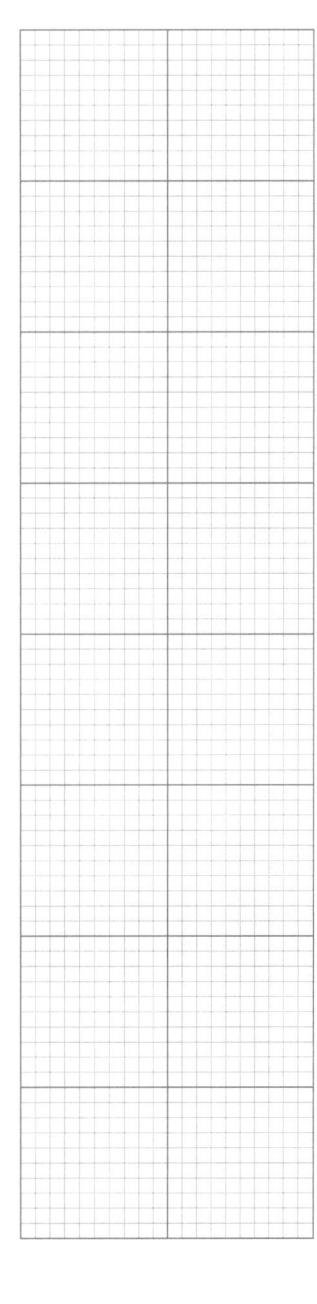

Practice question 12

The masses of different volumes of lithium are shown in Table 3.11.

Volume cm^3	Mass g
0	0
1	0.6
2	1.0
3	1.6
4	2.2
5	3.0

Table 3.11 Masses of different volumes of lithium

Draw suitable axes for a line graph to show these data values.

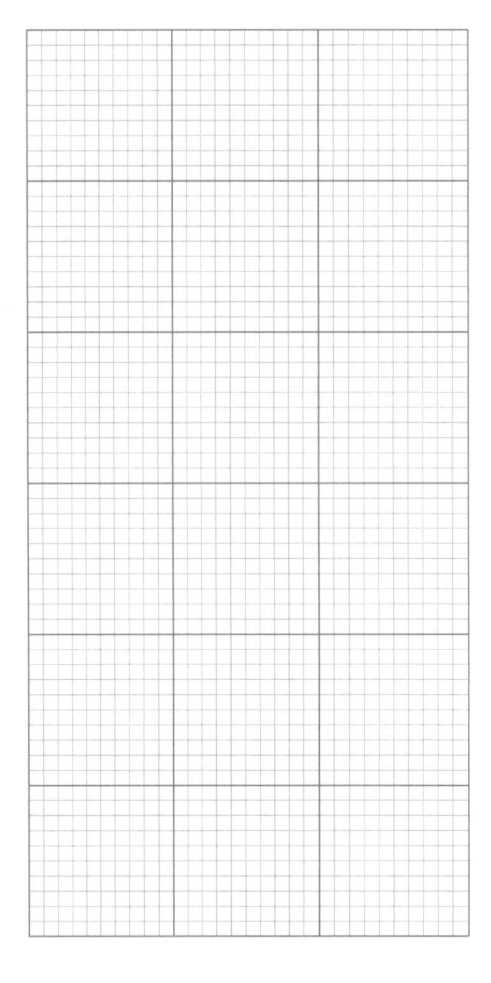

Chapter 3: Drawing charts and graphs

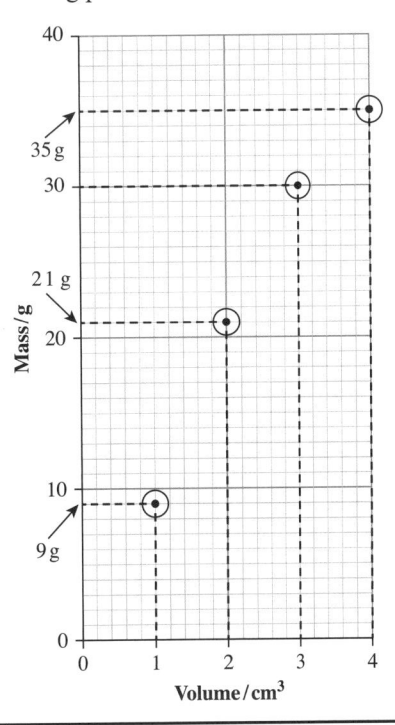

TIP

To find the values you need to work out the value of a small square. This is equal to the value of a large square divided by 10. In this example, one tiny square along the vertical axis is equal to $\frac{10}{10} = 1\,g$.

WORKED EXAMPLE 7

Maths skill 3: Plotting the data points

A student measures the masses of different volumes of copper. Her data are shown in the table below.

Plot her data points on a grid with the axes drawn earlier in Worked Example 6, Maths skill 2.

Volume cm³	Mass g
0	0
1	9
2	21
3	30
4	35

Step 1 Find the values of a pair of measurements on the axes.

Find the value of each independent variable on the horizontal axis and the corresponding value of the dependent variable on the vertical axis.

Step 2 Find the point where they coincide and mark with a dot.

To do this, track vertically upwards from the value on the horizontal axis and horizontally across from the value on the vertical axis. Mark a small dot where the tracks **intersect**.

Step 3 Either draw a small circle around this dot or mark a small cross with the centre exactly over the dot.

Repeat for the remaining points.

53

Practice question 13

The masses of different volumes of caesium are shown in Table 3.12.

Plot the data points on the axes that you drew in Maths skill 2, Practice question 11.

Volume cm³	Mass g
0	0
1	1.9
2	3.8
3	5.7
4	7.6

Table 3.12 Masses of different volumes of caesium

Practice question 14

The masses of different volumes of lithium are shown in Table 3.13.

Plot the data points on the axes that you drew in Maths skill 2, Practice question 12.

Volume cm³	Mass g
0	0
1	0.6
2	1.0
3	1.6
4	2.2
5	3.0

Table 3.13 Masses of different volumes of lithium

Chapter 3: Drawing charts and graphs

Maths skill 4: Using a ruler to draw a best-fit line

WORKED EXAMPLE 8

The graph in Figure 3.9 shows the masses of different volumes of copper. Draw a line of best fit.

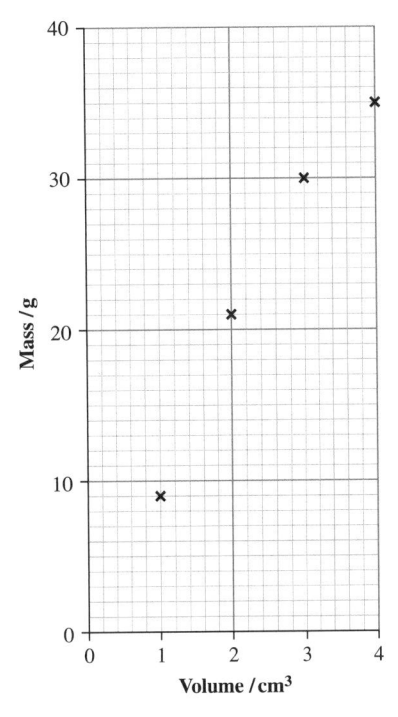

Figure 3.9 Masses of different volumes of copper

Step 1 Place a transparent ruler roughly in line with the points.

Think about whether the line should pass through the origin (0, 0). Does it make sense?

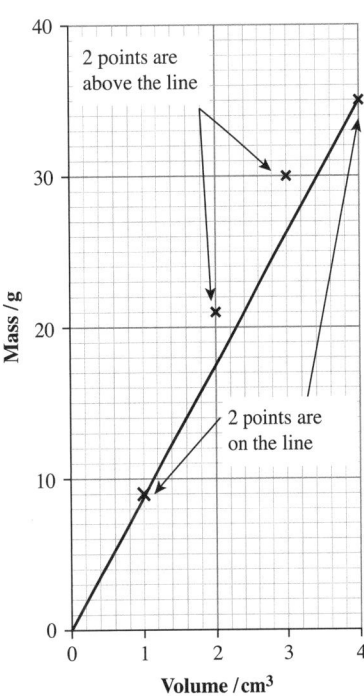

Step 2 Adjust the ruler to ensure a best-fit line.

Adjust the position of the ruler until there are roughly the same number of points, evenly spread, above and below the line. Sometimes a point does not fit the pattern. It is an outlier. Outliers should be ignored when drawing a line of best fit.

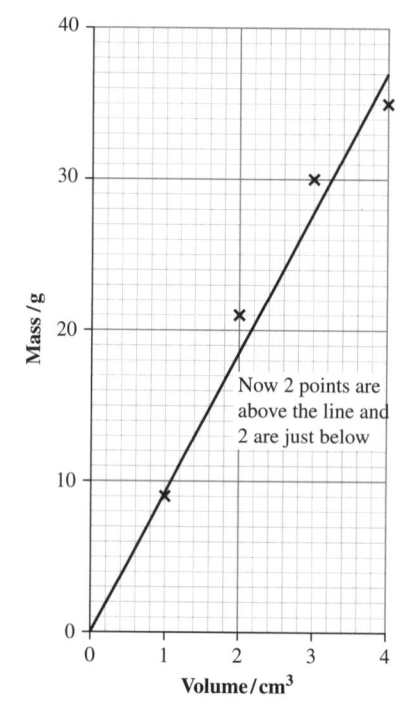

Now 2 points are above the line and 2 are just below

Step 3 Draw the line carefully – use a sharp pencil.

Practice question 15

The graph below shows the masses of different volumes of lead. Draw a line of best fit.

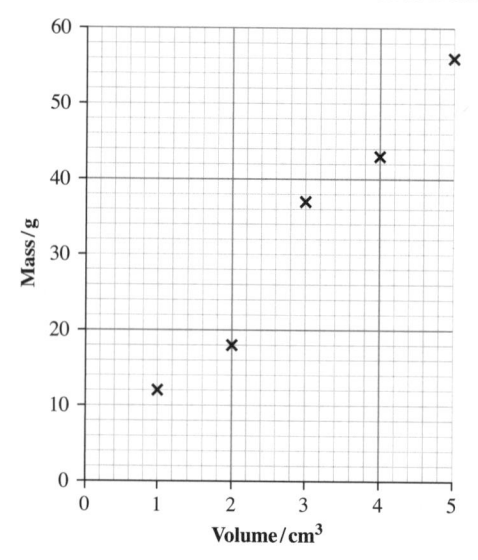

Practice question 16

The graph below shows the masses of different volumes of iron. Draw a line of best fit.

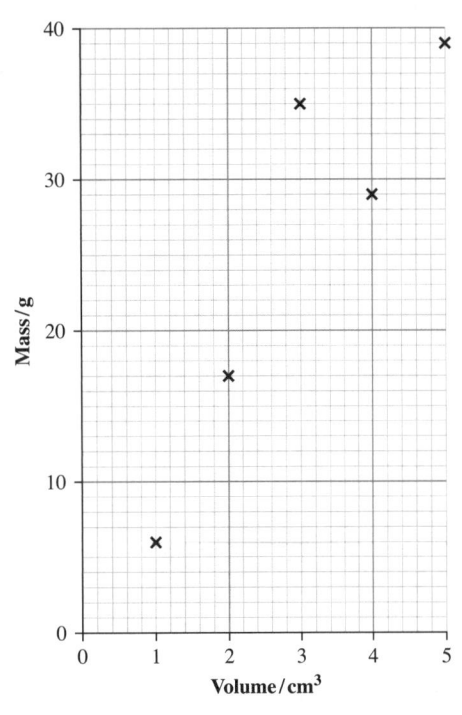

Maths skill 5: Drawing a best-fit curve freehand

WORKED EXAMPLE 9

The graph below shows the volume of hydrogen produced each minute when magnesium reacts with hydrochloric acid. Draw a best-fit curve.

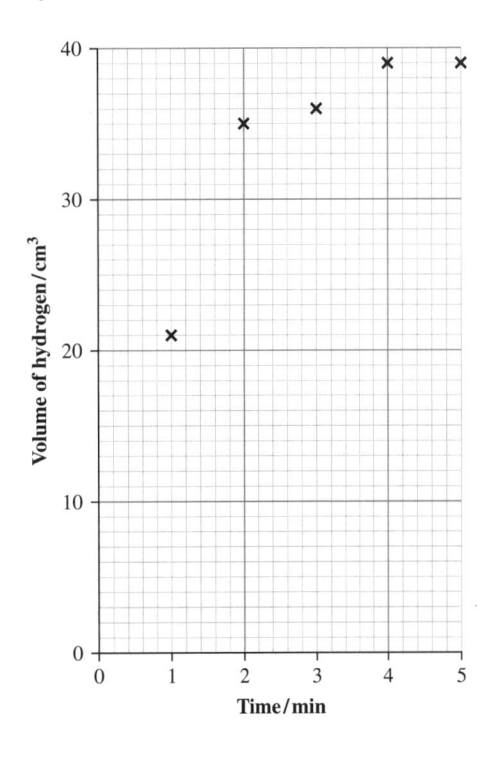

Step 1 Picture the shape of the curve.

Look at the graph and try to picture the shape of the curve formed by the points. Think about whether the curve should pass through the origin (0, 0).

Ignore any outliers.

Step 2 Practise drawing the curve.

Using a sweeping movement of the hand (with the wrist or elbow as a pivot), practise drawing a smooth curve without marking the paper.

Make sure the points are distributed roughly evenly on either side of the curve, along its whole length.

Step 3 When you are sure of where you want the curve to go, move your hand with the sweeping movement that you practised and (using a sharp pencil) draw the curve.

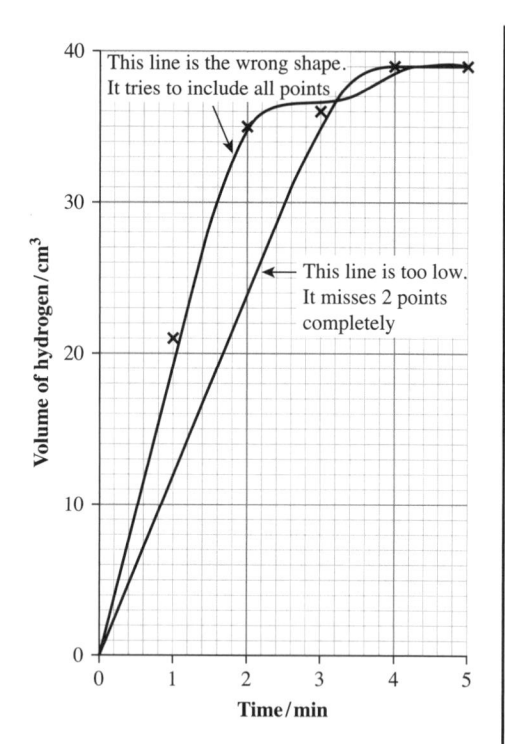

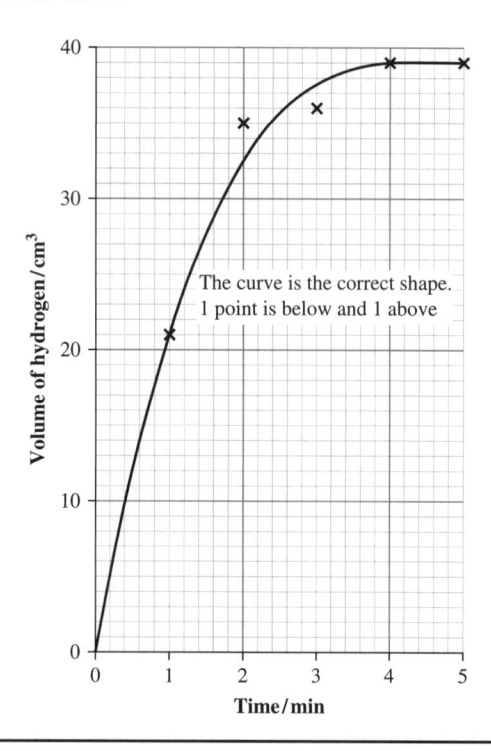

Practice question 17

Hydrogen peroxide (H_2O_2) gradually decomposes (slowly breaks down) into water and oxygen. This can be speeded up by the addition of a catalyst.

The graph shows the volume of oxygen produced every 10 seconds when a catalyst is added to hydrogen peroxide.

Draw the best-fit curve.

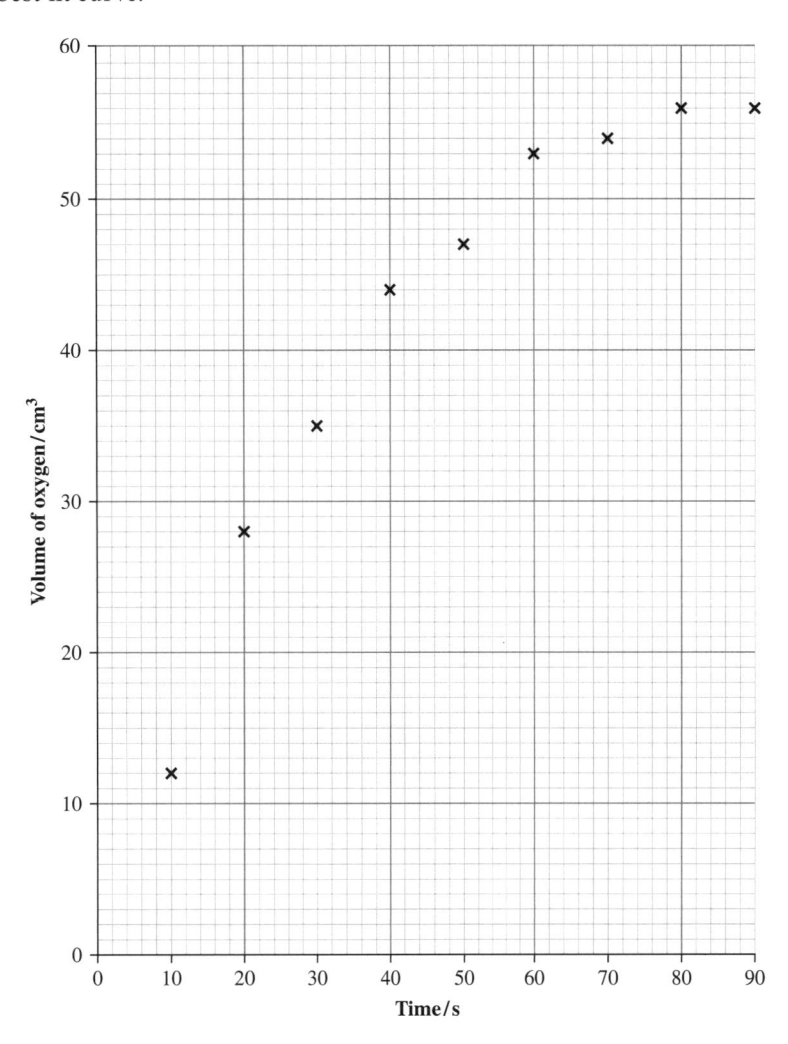

Practice question 18

A beaker containing hydrochloric acid is placed on a balance and some marble chips are added. The mass is recorded every minute and the data plotted on the graph below.

Draw a curved line of best fit.

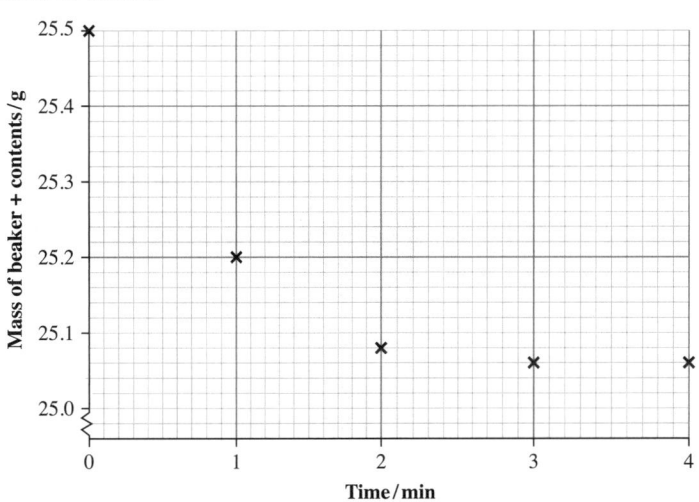

WATCH OUT

It is important to choose the correct range of the vertical axis of the graph. In this case the axis starts at 25.0 g. If the range is too large the shape of the curve may not be clearly seen.

TIP

The zig-zag on the bottom of the vertical axis indicates that the scale does not start at zero.

Further questions

1 The elements in Group 6 of the Periodic Table can all form compounds with hydrogen.

   a i Use the data below to draw a bar chart comparing the melting points of these hydrogen compounds.

Compound	Melting point °C
H_2O	0
H_2S	−85
H_2Se	−60
H_2Te	−49

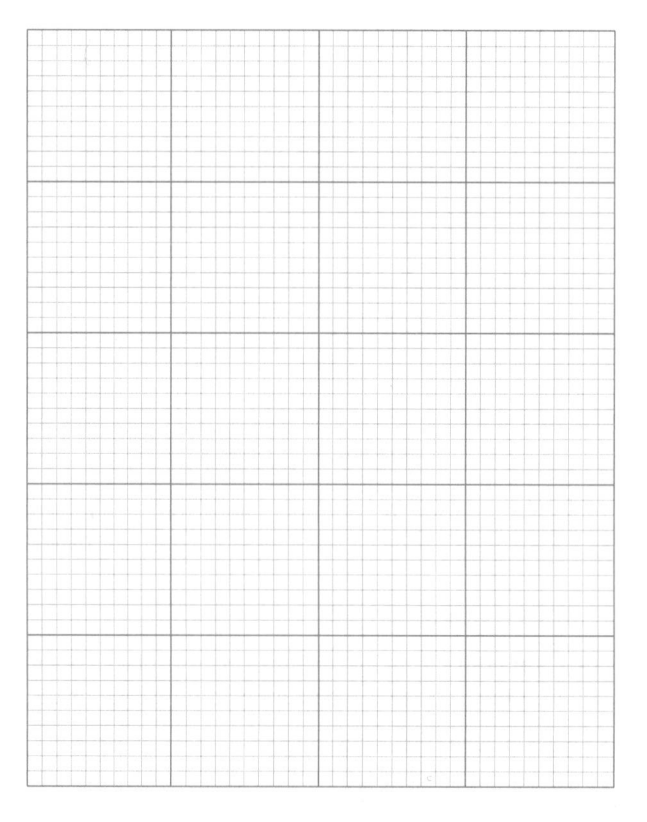

   ii Use the data below to draw a bar chart to compare the boiling points of the same compounds.

Compound	Boiling point °C
H_2O	100
H_2S	−61
H_2Se	−41
H_2Te	−2

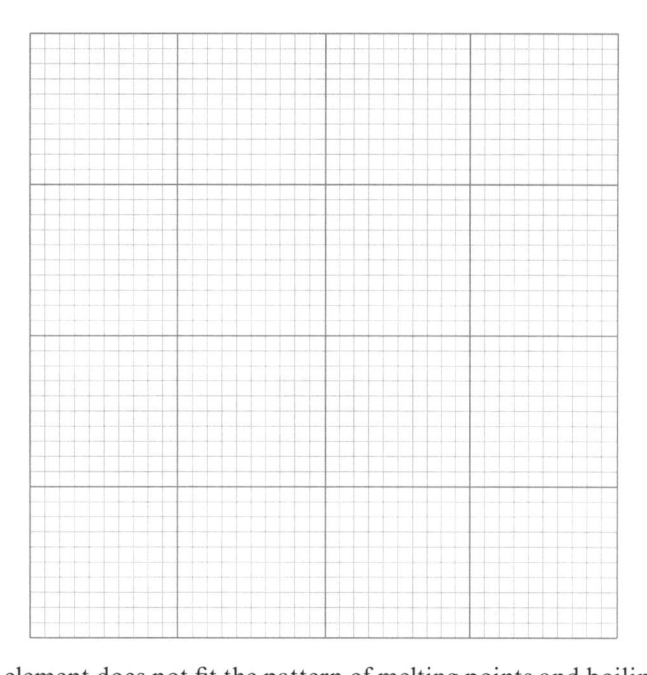

b i Which element does not fit the pattern of melting points and boiling points of Group 6?

....

ii Explain why not fitting this pattern is critical for life on Earth.

....

....

2 The data below show the percentage of copper in three different types of copper mineral. Each mineral is made of a different compound of copper and sulfur.

a Complete the table below to show the percentage of sulfur in each mineral.

Ore	Percentage of copper (rounded to nearest whole number)	Percentage of sulfur
Covellite, CuS	67	
Chalcocite, Cu_2S	80	
Digenite, Cu_9S_5	78	

b Draw a pie chart to show the percentage composition of the ore with the greatest percentage of copper.

c Explain which type of chart is best for comparing the percentage of copper in the ores.

....

....

....

3 The maximum mass of a salt that dissolves in 100 g of water is called its *solubility*. Solubility changes with temperature. This can be seen clearly on a line graph.

  a Draw axes and plot points to show the data below.

Temperature °C	Solubility of copper sulfate in 100 g water g
0	14
10	17
20	21
30	30
40	29
50	32
60	42
70	47
80	56

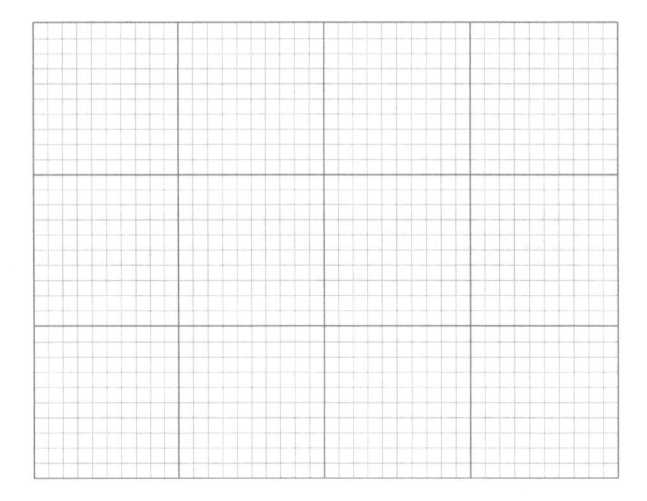

  b Draw a line or curve of best fit. (Circle any **anomalous results**.)

Chapter 4:
Interpreting data

Why do you need to interpret data in chemistry?

Collecting data during an experiment is meaningless unless you interpret it, to find out what it means.

It is much easier to identify patterns and relationships between variables if you plot the data as a chart or graph.

Types of graph used in chemistry

Bar charts help you to compare the values of the different categories of the data.

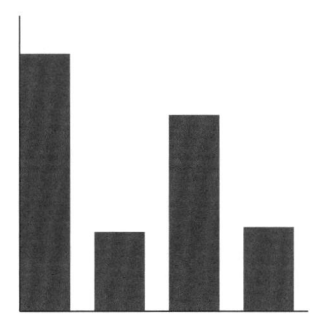

Figure 4.1 A bar chart

Pie charts give a visual comparison of the percentages of the different categories that make up the whole.

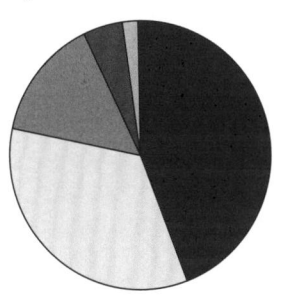

Figure 4.2 A pie chart

A line graph can show you more about the relationship between variables (how the variables are connected).

Some variables in chemistry may have a linear relationship. Points along a best-fit line are closer to the true values than the points plotted from the measured values. Usually the line passes through the origin, where the axes cross and the value of both variables is zero, but it does not have to.

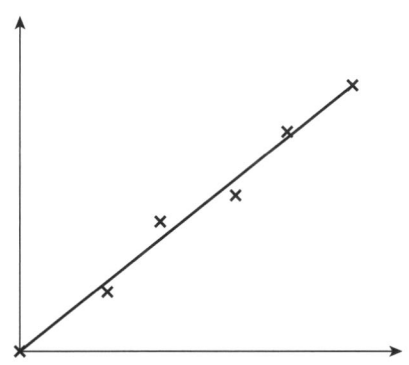

> **LINK**
> See Chapter 3, Maths focus 3, 'Drawing line graphs' for more on best-fit lines and curves.

Figure 4.3 A line graph with a best-fit line

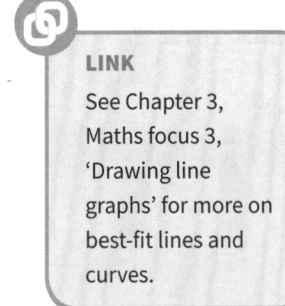

Not all variables have a linear relationship. Some may form a curved line when plotted on a graph. A best-fit curve is drawn instead of a best-fit line.

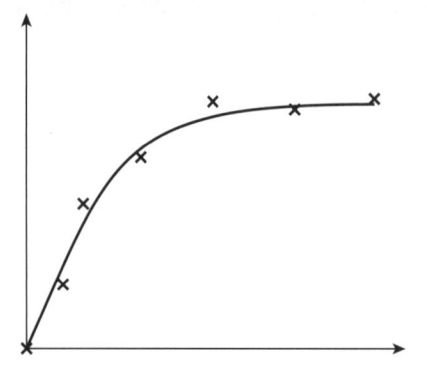

Figure 4.4 A best-fit curve

Maths focus 1: Interpreting charts

Bar charts and pie charts show categories of data, but in different ways.

The heights of the bars on a bar chart represent the values of the categories of data.

The bar chart in Figure 4.5 compares the energy produced (per gram) when burning different types of fuel.

The height of the bar shows the energy produced (per gram) when burning this type of fuel

Values shown on bars: 143, 56, 48, 33, 30, 23, 16, 10

Fuels (x-axis): hydrogen gas, H_2; methane gas, CH_4; petrol (octane), C_8H_{18}; coal (carbon), C; ethanol, C_2H_5OH; methanol, CH_3OH; carbohydrates, e.g. glucose, $C_6H_{12}O_6$; carbon monoxide gas, CO

y-axis: Energy produced by burning kJ/g

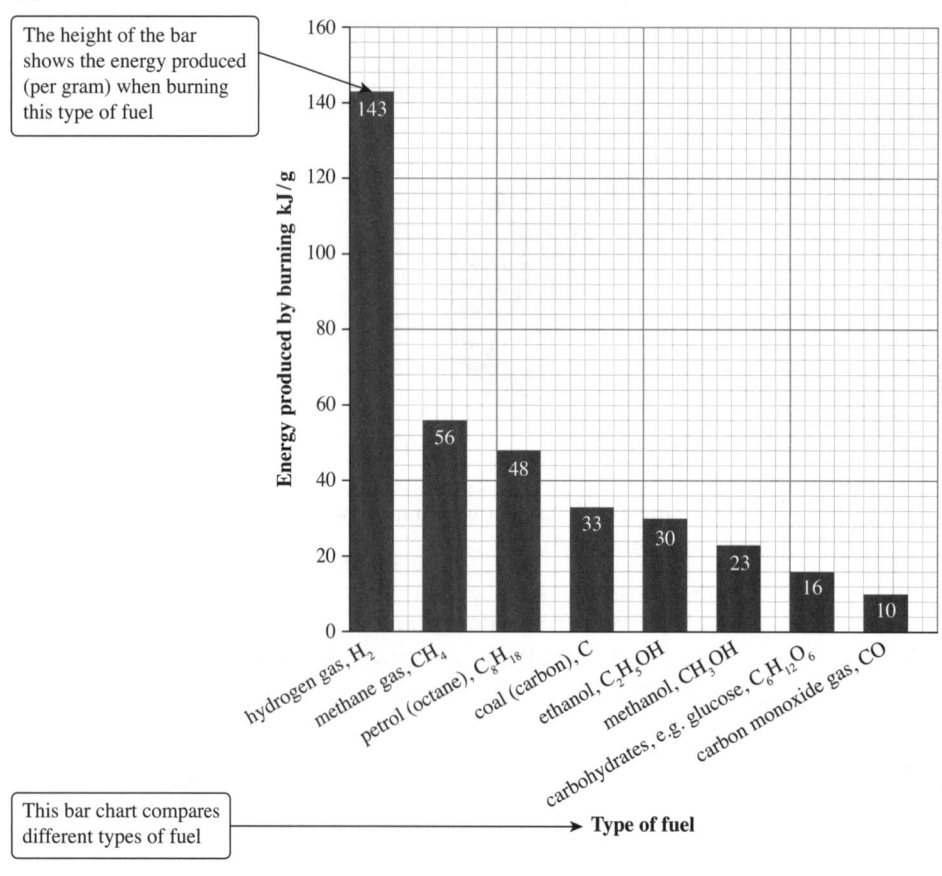

This bar chart compares different types of fuel → Type of fuel

Figure 4.5 Energy produced from different types of fuel

Chapter 4: Interpreting data

The sectors on a pie chart allow you to compare the percentages of the whole represented by each category of data.

The pie chart in Figure 4.6 shows the percentages of different types of gas in Earth's atmosphere.

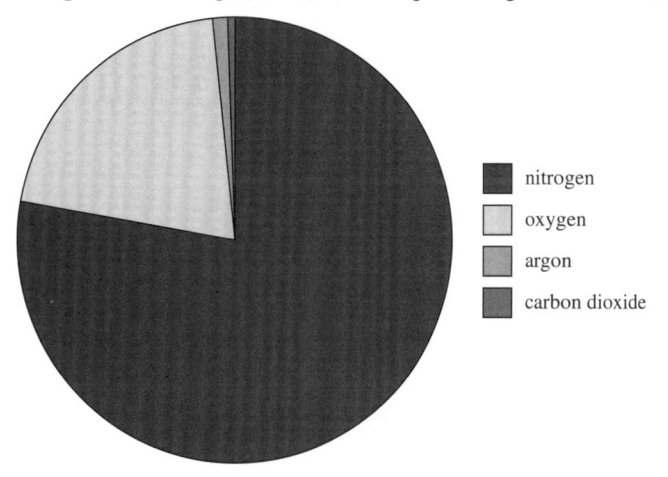

- nitrogen
- oxygen
- argon
- carbon dioxide

Figure 4.6 Percentages of gases in the Earth's atmosphere

What maths skills do you need to interpret charts?

1	Interpreting the heights of bars on a bar chart	• Identify any patterns • Work out the scale on the vertical axis • Compare the height of the bars numerically
2	Comparing sizes of sectors on a pie chart	• **Estimate** percentages shown for the larger sectors • List the categories included in the smallest sector

Maths skills practice

How does interpreting charts help you to compare environmental data?

Charts can be used to display a wide range of data that can help you to make decisions about how to reduce negative impacts on the environment.

A bar chart can be used to compare categories, such as the quantities of different types of material that are recycled or the numbers of cars produced that use different fuels.

Bar graphs are also useful for showing trends over a number of years.

Pie charts can help you to compare percentages and answer questions such as:

'Of all the waste that is recycled, what percentage is made of plastic? What percentage is card?'

or, 'Of all the cars produced, what percentage are diesel? What percentage are petrol? What percentage are electric?'

Maths skill 1: Interpreting the heights of bars on a bar chart

WORKED EXAMPLE 1

The bar chart in Figure 4.7 shows the percentage of each type of waste that is recycled.

a Describe any patterns shown in the bar chart.

b Find the highest and lowest percentage recycled.

WATCH OUT

In this example, the percentages cannot be shown on a pie chart. They do not add up to 100% because they are percentages of different categories of waste materials.

c Calculate the difference between the highest and lowest percentage recycled.

A bar chart to show the percentage of different types of waste that are recycled

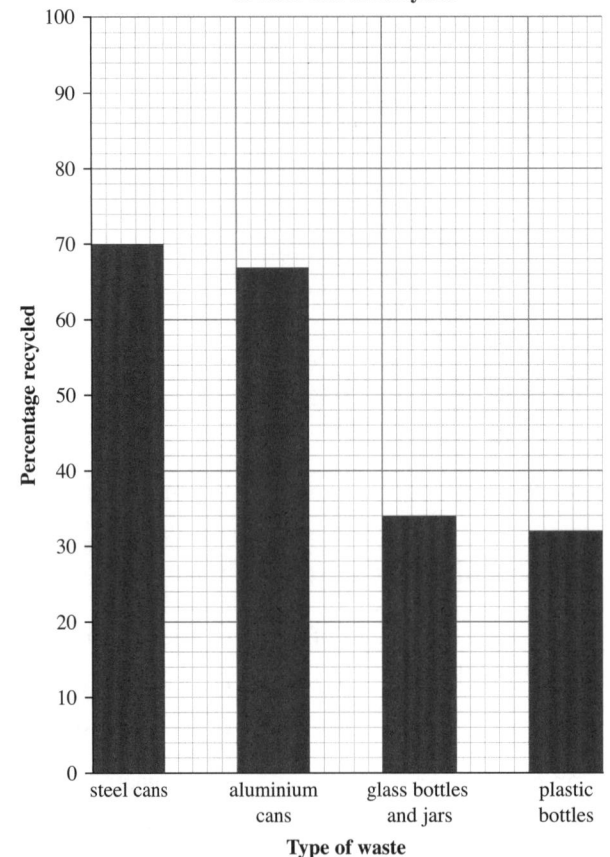

[Bar chart showing: steel cans ≈ 70%, aluminium cans ≈ 67%, glass bottles and jars ≈ 34%, plastic bottles ≈ 32%. Y-axis: Percentage recycled (0–100). X-axis: Type of waste.]

Figure 4.7 Waste that can be recycled

Step 1 Identify any patterns.

    a In this bar chart, the two bars for steel cans and aluminium are roughly equal and show roughly twice the percentage of glass bottles and jars or plastic bottles (which are about the same). The bar chart does not show a trend in terms of a steady increase or decrease, but this is to be expected with categorical data like this.

Step 2 Work out the scale used on the vertical axis.

    b The scale used is one large square for every 20%.

Step 3 Compare the height of the bars numerically.

The category of waste with the highest percentage recycled is shown by the tallest bar (steel cans) and that with the lowest percentage by the shortest bar (plastic bottles). Tracking across horizontally from the top of each bar to read the value on the vertical axis (on the left) shows that the highest percentage recycled is 70% (of steel cans). The lowest percentage is 32% (plastic bottles).

    c The difference between the highest and lowest percentages recycled is 70 − 32 = 38%. This shows that another 38% of plastic bottles need to be recycled in order to match recycling levels of steel cans.

TIP

Trends are more likely to appear in bar charts where the categories are based on years, because these bar charts show changes over time. For example, changes in pollution levels over a century.

Chapter 4: Interpreting data

Practice question 1

The bar chart in Figure 4.8 shows the total numbers of electric and hybrid cars produced each year.

a Describe any patterns shown in the bar chart.

....

....

b Find the highest and lowest numbers of cars produced.

....

....

c Calculate by how much the number of cars produced increased from 2010 to 2014.

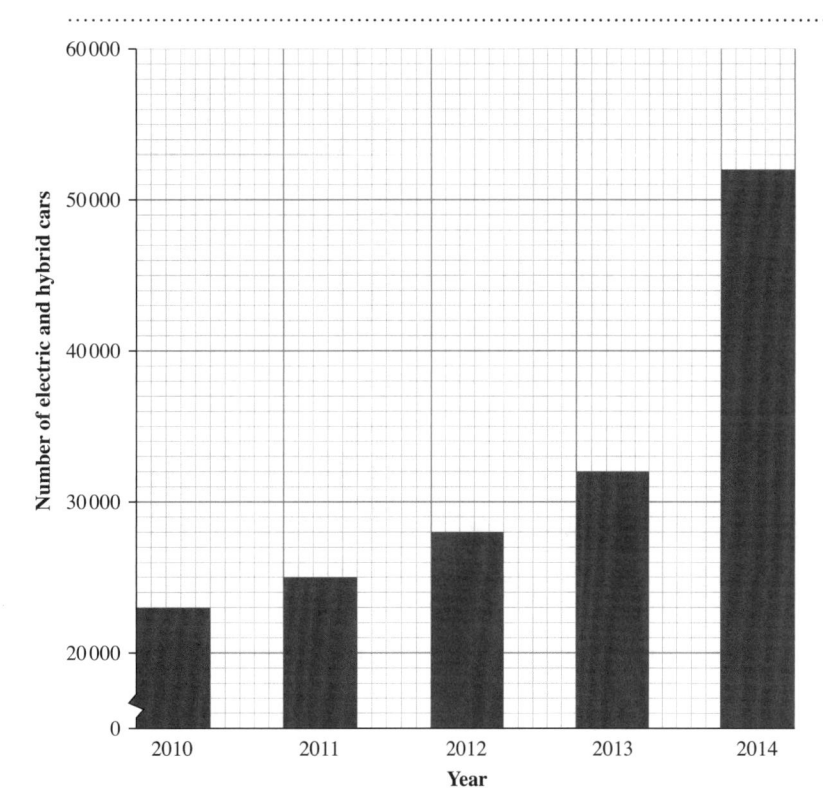

....

Figure 4.8 The total numbers of electric and hybrid cars produced each year

Maths skill 2: Comparing sizes of sectors on a pie chart

It helps if you can easily recognise key percentages as fractions of a whole circle, see Table 4.1.

$\frac{1}{4}$	$\frac{1}{3}$	$\frac{1}{2}$	$\frac{3}{4}$	$\frac{1}{10}$	$\frac{1}{20}$
25%	$33\frac{1}{3}$%	50%	75%	10%	5%

Table 4.1 Key percentages of a circle

Cambridge IGCSE Chemistry Maths Skills

> **TIP**
> Categories with very small percentages are often combined into one sector because the angles required are too small to be drawn clearly. The categories should be identified in the key or labelled.

WORKED EXAMPLE 2

The pie chart in Figure 4.9 shows the percentages of water in different types of water-based environment found on Earth.

a   Identify the type of environment that holds the largest percentage of water.

b   Estimate the percentage of water found as this type.

c   List the types of environment where the smallest percentages of water are found.

Key:
- ice and snow
- lakes
- soil moisture
- swamps and marshes
- rivers, biological and atmospheric water

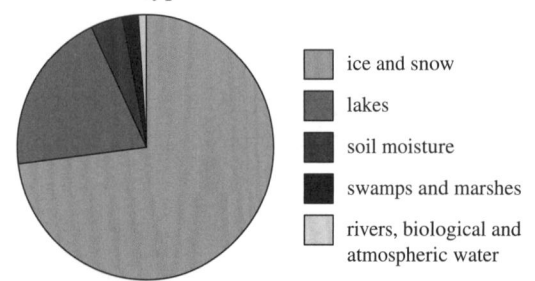

Figure 4.9 Percentages of water in different water-based environments

Step 1   Find the category represented by the largest sector.

   a   The largest sector is 'ice and snow'.

Step 2   Estimate the percentage represented by the largest sector.

   b   The percentage of 'ice and snow' is just under 75%.

Step 3   Find the category represented by the smallest sector.

   c   The smallest sector includes rivers, biological water and atmospheric water.

Practice question 2

The pie chart in Figure 4.10 shows the percentages of water contained in different types of freshwater environment.

a   Identify the environment that holds the largest percentage of fresh water.

   ....

b   Estimate the percentage of fresh water found in this environment type.

   ....

c   Identify the type of environment where the smallest percentage of fresh water is found.

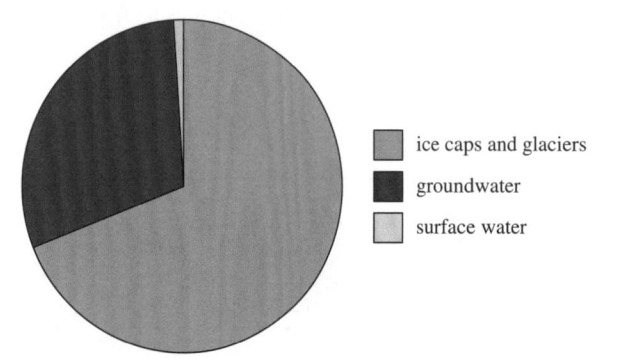

   ....

Key:
- ice caps and glaciers
- groundwater
- surface water

Figure 4.10 Percentages of water in different freshwater environments

Chapter 4: Interpreting data

Maths focus 2: Reading values from a line graph

When you draw a line graph you use a fixed set of data. Once you have drawn the best-fit line or curve you can work out values between your data points. For example, if you measured the mass of a substance with volume $1\,cm^3$, $2\,cm^3$, $3\,cm^3$ and $4\,cm^3$ then you can use the graph to find out the mass of the same substance with volume $1.5\,cm^3$. This is called **interpolation**.

Suppose you need to find out a value such as the mass for $6\,cm^3$, which lies outside the range of those that have been measured, then you need to extend or **extrapolate** the graph. It is easy to extend a best-fit line and then read off the values, as before. This is called extrapolation.

What maths skills do you need to read values from a line graph?

1	Interpolating line graphs	• Start with the known independent value, read up to the best-fit line, then across to the dependent axis
		• Start with the known dependent value, read across to the best-fit line, then down to the independent axis
2	Extrapolating line graphs	• Place a ruler along the line and draw the extension
		• Use the extended line to find values beyond those actually measured

Maths skills practice

How does reading values from a graph help to interpret data about rates of reaction?

Data from an experiment investigating the rate of formation of a product (or loss of a reactant) during a reaction often show a non-linear relationship. This makes it more difficult to determine mathematically values that have not been directly measured. However, it is easy to read values off the graph once a curve of best fit has been drawn.

Maths skill 1: Interpolating line graphs

WORKED EXAMPLE 3

The graph below shows the masses of different volumes of lead. Use the graph to find:

a the mass of $2\,cm^3$ of lead

b the volume of $50\,g$ of lead.

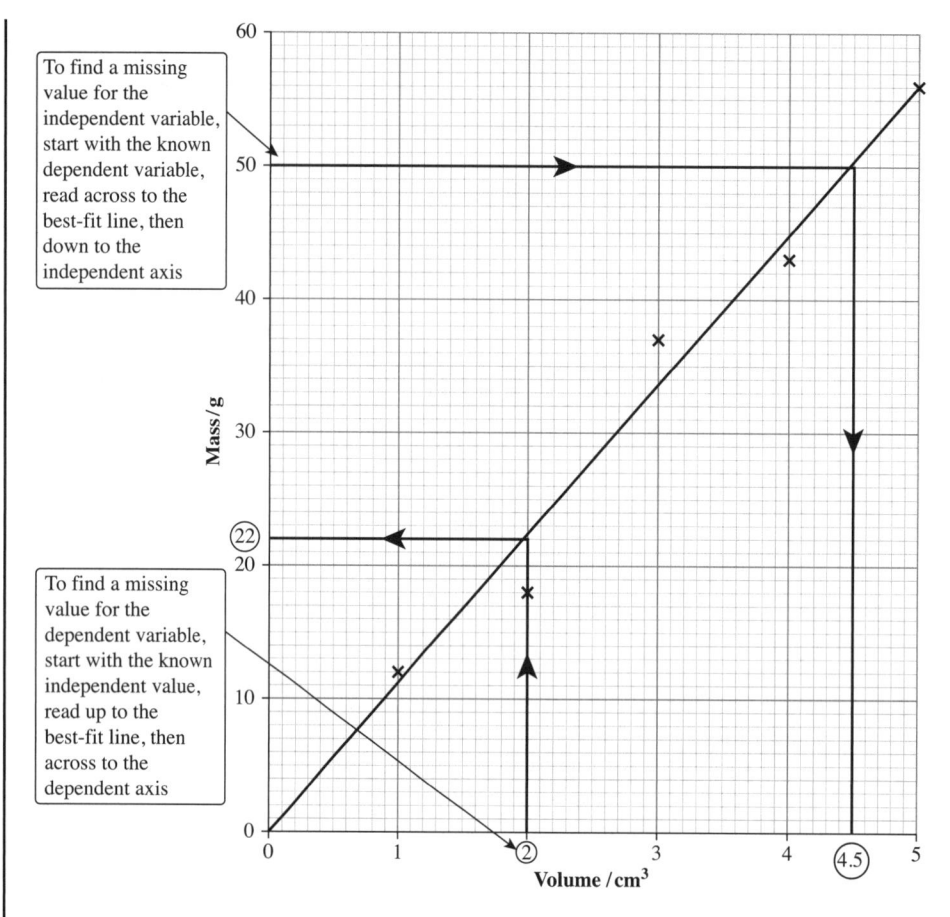

Cambridge IGCSE Chemistry Maths Skills

TIP
It is often more accurate to read a value from the best-fit line than from a data point that lies above or below the line, as the best-fit line 'smooths out' inaccuracies in the measurements.

To find a missing value for the independent variable, start with the known dependent variable, read across to the best-fit line, then down to the independent axis

To find a missing value for the dependent variable, start with the known independent value, read up to the best-fit line, then across to the dependent axis

Reading from the graph:

a the mass of 2 cm3 of lead is 22 g

b the volume of 50 g of lead is 4.5 cm³

Practice question 3

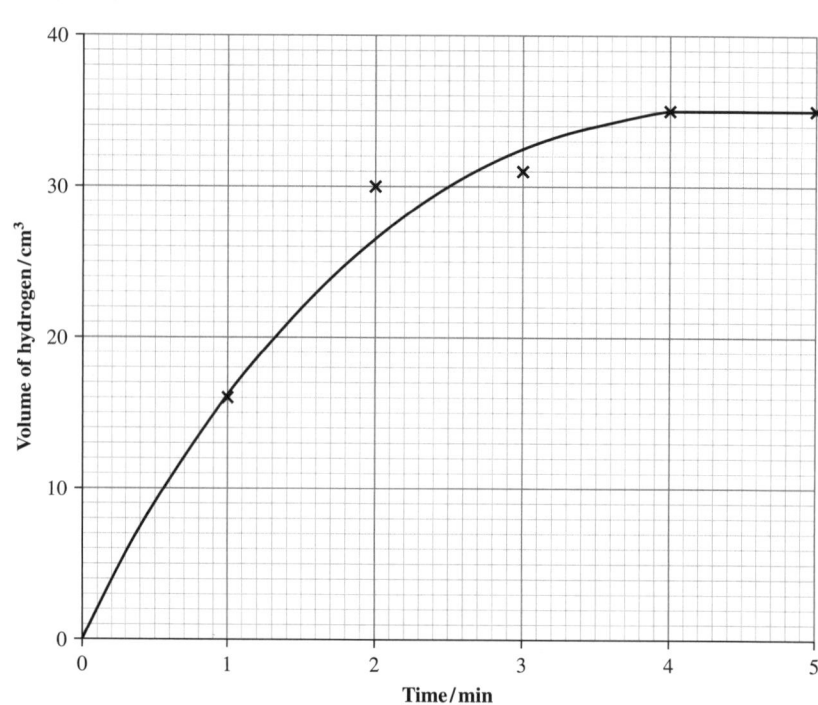

TIP
You can read values from a curved line in exactly the same way as for a straight line.

The graph below shows the volume of hydrogen produced during a reaction between hydrochloric acid and magnesium.

Use the graph to find:

a the volume of hydrogen produced after 0.5 minutes ....

b the volume of hydrogen produced after 1.5 minutes ....

c the time taken to produce 30 cm³ of hydrogen ....

d the time taken to produce 34 cm³ of hydrogen. ....

Maths skill 2: Extrapolating line graphs

WORKED EXAMPLE 4

The graph below shows the masses of different volumes of iron.

a What is the mass of 7 cm³ of iron?

b What is the volume of 45 g of iron?

Step 1 Place a ruler along the line and draw the extension.

Step 2 Use the extended line to find values beyond those actually measured.

Reading from the extended graph:

a a volume of 7 cm³ of iron has a mass of 53 g

b a mass of 45 g of iron has a volume of 6 cm³

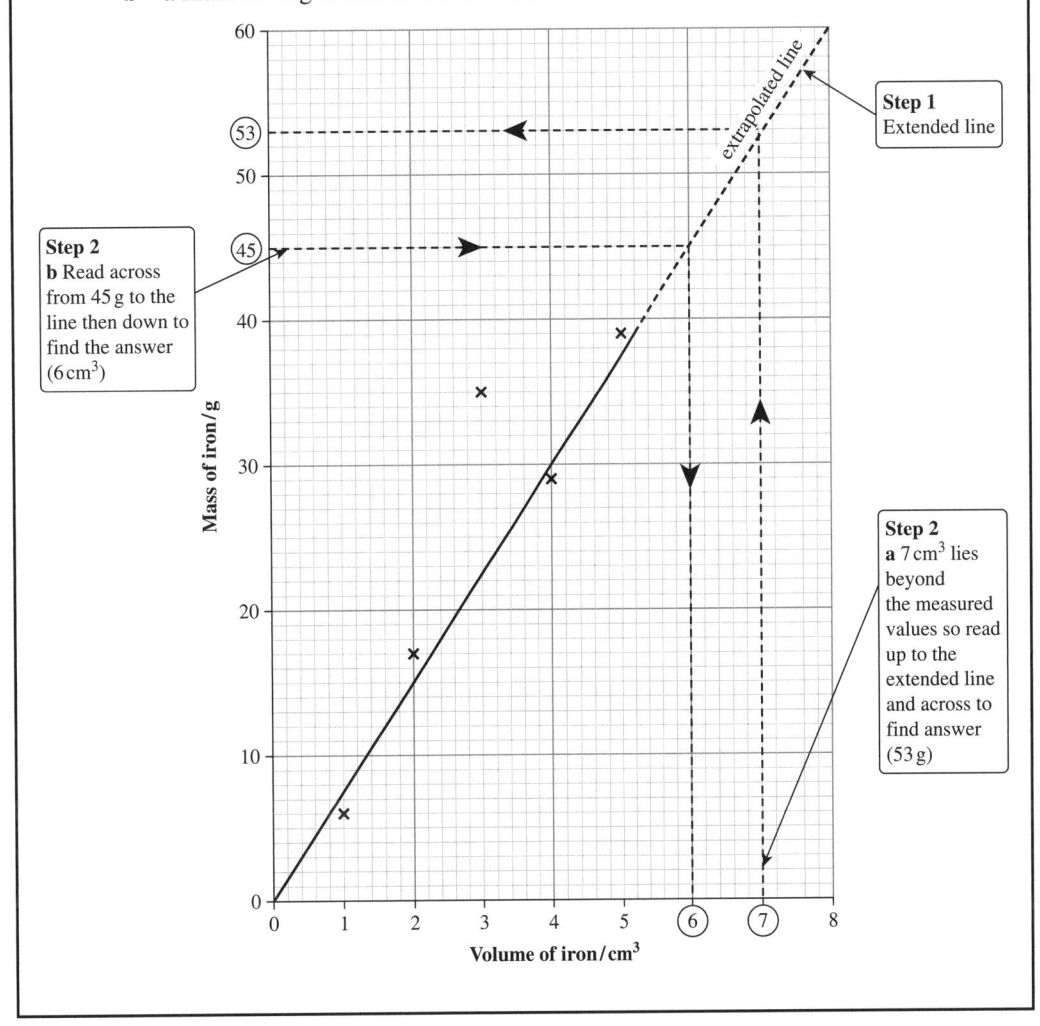

TIP
Line graphs can also be extrapolated to find smaller values.

Step 1 Extended line

Step 2
b Read across from 45 g to the line then down to find the answer (6 cm³)

Step 2
a 7 cm³ lies beyond the measured values so read up to the extended line and across to find answer (53 g)

Practice question 4

The graph shows the masses of different volumes of copper. Use it to find:

a the mass of 5 cm³ of copper ....

b the mass of 6 cm³ of copper ....

c the volume of 50 g of copper ....

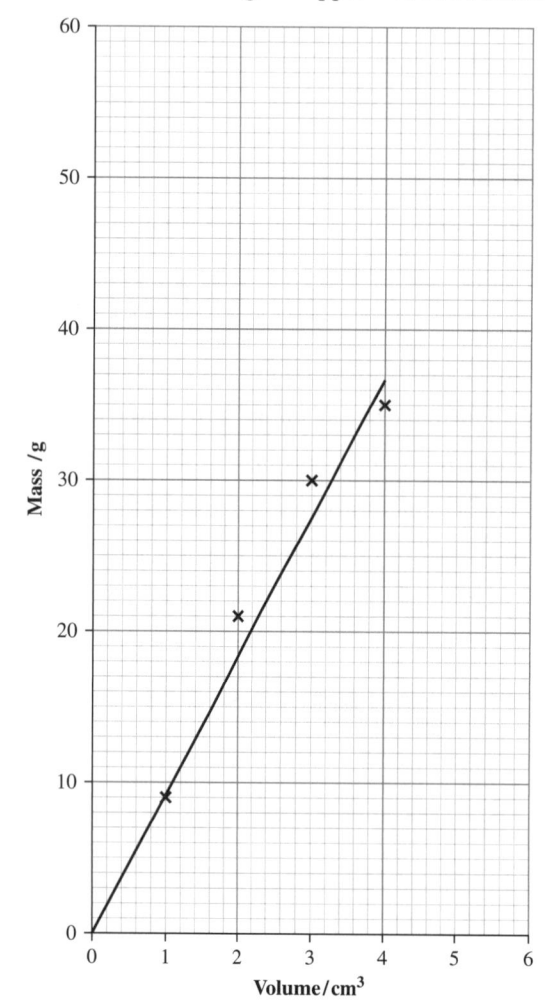

Maths focus 3: Interpreting the shape of line graphs

A line graph can give you information without referring to the numbers on the axes.

The shape of a graph shows you the relationship between the variables on the horizontal axis and the vertical axis.

The **gradient** (slope) of a line graph can have a scientific meaning, such as the rate of a reaction.

The gradient of a straight-line graph is constant. If you need a numerical value for the gradient of a straight-line graph, you can use values from the graph to calculate it.

Figure 4.11 The gradient of a ramp

The slope of the straight ramp in Figure 4.11 remains the same.

Chapter 4: Interpreting data

The gradient of a curved line graph changes.

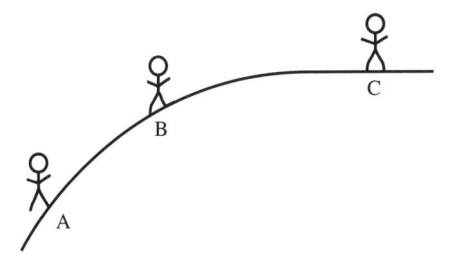

Figure 4.12 The gradient of a hill

The slope of the hill in Figure 4.12 changes from A to C. The gradient at point A is greater than the gradient at point B.

At the top of the hill (point C) the ground is flat, so the gradient is zero.

By looking at how the gradient changes at different places on a curved line graph, you can find out and describe how this quantity changes at different points; for example, how a rate of reaction changes with time.

> **TIP**
> A **rate** of change is a measure of how quickly a variable changes. For example, a rate of reaction could be determined by how much the volume of a gaseous product increases each minute.

What maths skills do you need to interpret the shape of line graphs?

1	Recognising the shape of the graph	• Categorise the relationship from the shape of the graph, as **directly proportional**, **inversely proportional** or neither state if the graph reaches a maximum or minimum.
2	Interpreting the changing gradient of a curve	• Describe how the gradient (slope) changes at different points on a curved line graph • Link the gradient to a meaning in chemistry
3	Calculating the gradient of a straight-line graph	• Select two clear points along the line • Draw a right-angled triangle in which the line between these points forms the hypotenuse • Use the triangle to calculate the gradient. $$\text{gradient} = \frac{\text{change in vertical value}}{\text{change in horizontal value}}$$

> **LINK**
> See Chapter 2, Maths focus 2, Maths skill 1, 'Identifying the independent and dependent variables'.

Maths skills practice

How does recognising the shape of the graph give more information about the relationship between experimental variables?

Line graphs produced from experimental data show the *independent variable* on the horizontal axis and the *dependent variable* on the vertical axis.

If the line on the graph is sloping *upwards* (as in Figure 4.13) this tells you that as the value of the variable on the horizontal axis *increases*, the value of the variable on the vertical axis also increases (a **positive relationship**).

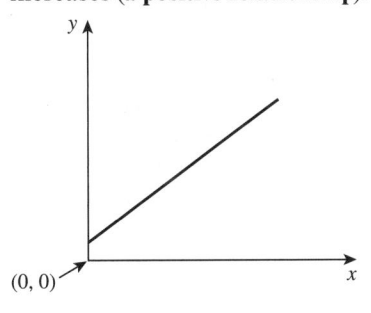

Figure 4.13 A positive relationship

If the line slopes *downwards* (as in Figure 4.14) then as the variable on the horizontal axis increases, the variable on the vertical axis *decreases* (a **negative relationship**).

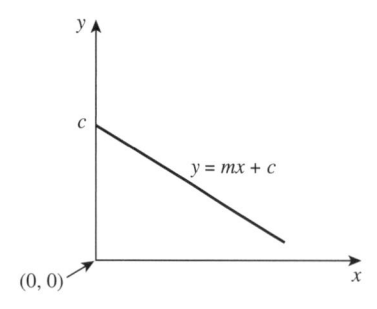

Figure 4.14 A negative relationship

If the relationship is linear it can be written in the form $y = mx + c$ where y is the dependent variable on the y-axis, x is the independent variable on the x-axis, m is the gradient (slope) and c is the y-**intercept** (where the line crosses the y-axis).

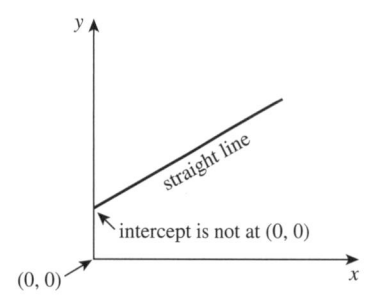

Figure 4.15 The y-intercept

This intercept is the value of the dependent variable when the value of the independent variable is zero (see Figure 4.15). For example, it could be the temperature of the reactants at the start of a reaction.

If the graph is a straight line passing through the origin (the intercept is 0) then the variables are said to be *directly proportional*, as in Figure 4.16. This means if a value of the variable on one axis is doubled then the value of the variable on the other is also doubled. In this case $y = mx$.

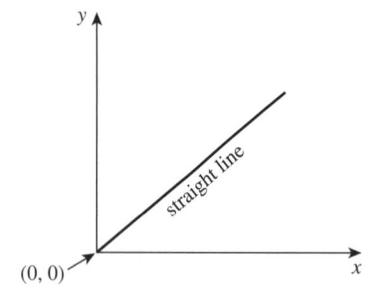

Figure 4.16 A directly proportional graph

If the graph is a curve, you can see that its gradient is continually changing, so the relationship between the variables is not linear.

If the variables are *inversely proportional*, as in Figure 4.17, then if the variable on one axis doubles the variable on the other axis halves. This is shown by a special type of curved graph, which approaches the axes but *never reaches* either of them.

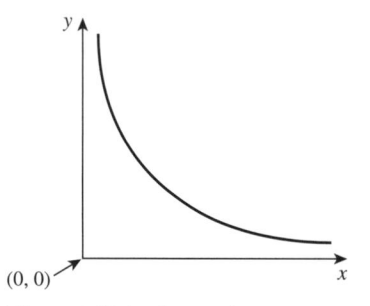

Figure 4.17 An inversely proportional graph

Some graphs show neither direct nor inverse proportionality, but they can still give you information about the variables, such as whether the variable on one axis is increasing or decreasing when the variable on the other axis increases.

If the steepness of a curved graph reduces so that the line becomes horizontal, this tells you that a maximum (or minimum) value is reached (see Figure 4.18).

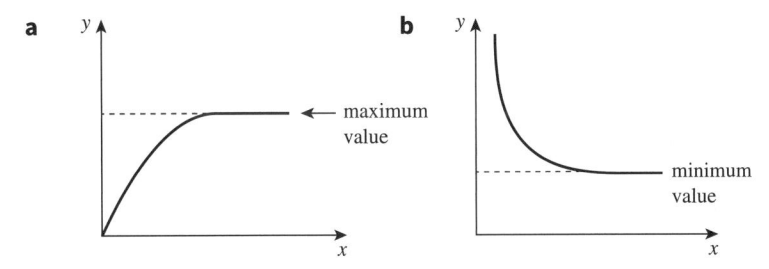

Figure 4.18 Graphs showing a) the maximum and b) the minimum values

Maths skill 1: Recognising the shape of the graph

WORKED EXAMPLE 5

The graph below shows how the volume of hydrogen produced in a reaction changes over time.

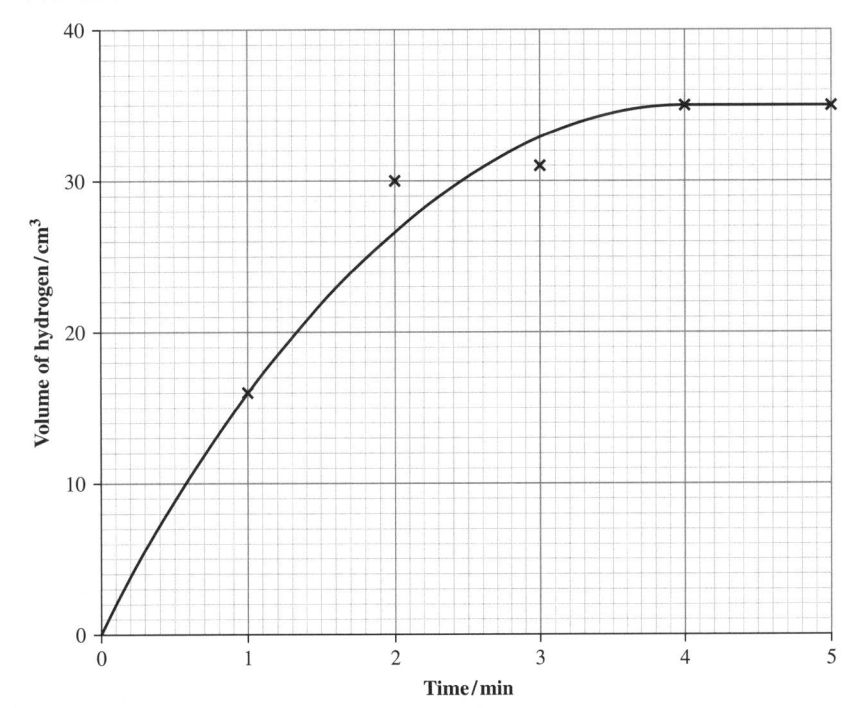

Match the graph to the description of the relationship between variables that it shows. Tick the correct one.

A The volume of hydrogen is directly proportional to time.

B Volume and time show a negative relationship.

C The volume of hydrogen reaches a maximum value. ✓

> **KEY QUESTIONS TO ASK YOURSELF:**
>
> - Is the graph a straight line?
>
>   The graph is not a straight line, which shows that the relationship is not linear. This means that the variables cannot be directly proportional.
>
> - Does the graph show an increase in the dependent variable as the independent variable increases?
>
>   The graph shows an increase over time so the variables do not show a negative relationship.
>
> - Does the graph become horizontal?
>
>   The line on the graph becomes horizontal so it shows that the volume of hydrogen reaches a maximum.

Practice question 5

For each graph, choose *two* statements from the table below that correctly describe the graph.

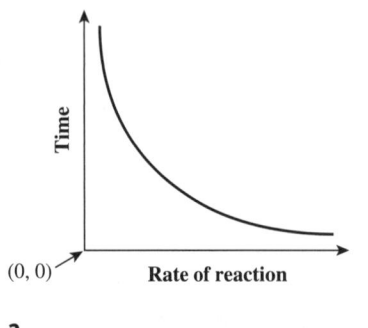

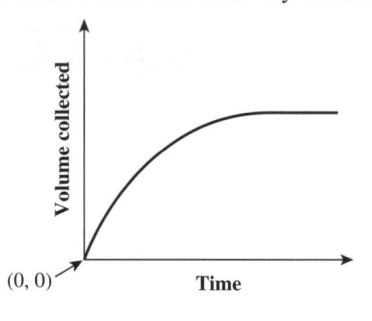

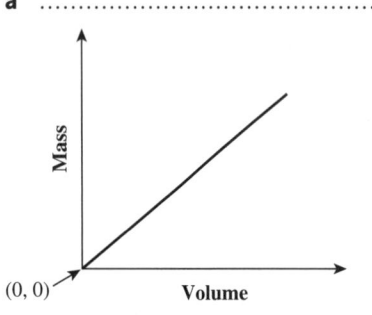

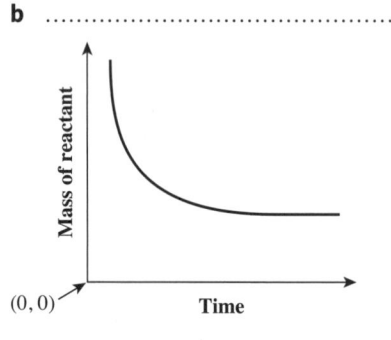

a ....

b ....

c ....

d ....

A	As the variable on the horizontal axis increases, the variable on the vertical axis increases.	B	As the variable on the horizontal axis increases, the variable on the vertical axis decreases.
C	The variables are directly proportional.	D	The variables are inversely proportional.
E	The graph reaches a maximum value.	F	The graph approaches a minimum value.

Chapter 4: Interpreting data

Maths skill 2: Interpreting the changing gradient of a curve

How does interpreting the gradient of a curved graph help to understand rates of reaction?

Interpreting the gradient of a curved graph can help to tell the 'story' of a reaction in terms of how the rate changes as the reaction progresses.

The rate of reaction at any time during the reaction is equal to the gradient of the graph at that point.

WORKED EXAMPLE 6

The graph below shows the volume of hydrogen produced as the reaction progresses. Describe how the graph shows how the rate of reaction changes during a reaction between magnesium and hydrochloric acid.

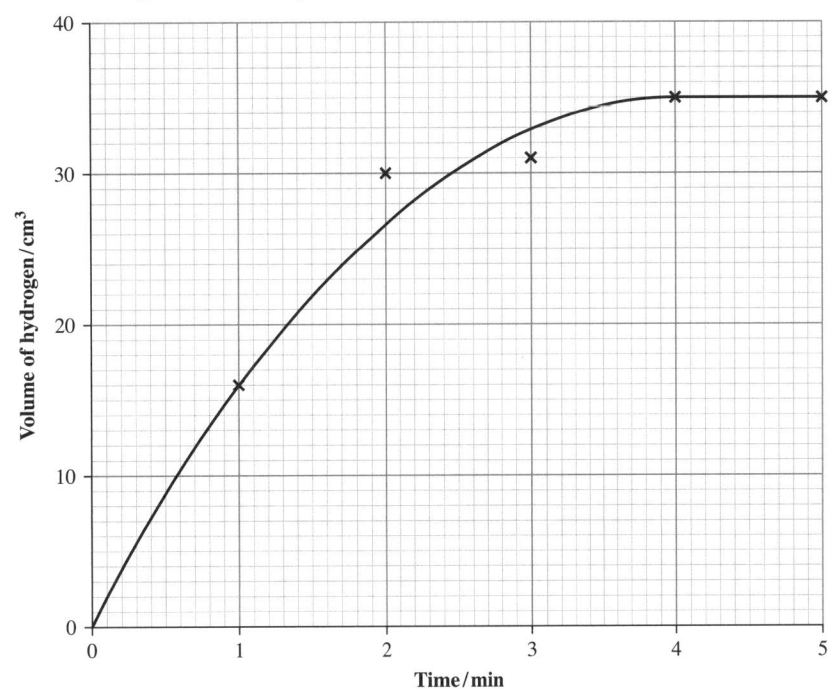

TIP
Imagine the curve represents a hill and that you are walking up the hill. Think about where the slope is steeper and where it is less steep.

Step 1 Describe how the gradient (slope) changes at different points on the graph.

The gradient of the graph is greatest at the start of the reaction. The gradient gradually decreases until about 4 minutes. Then the graph becomes horizontal, which means it has zero gradient.

Step 2 Link the gradient to a meaning in chemistry.

This means that the rate of reaction is fastest at the start and then gradually decreases until by 4 minutes the reaction stops.

Cambridge IGCSE Chemistry Maths Skills

Practice question 6

The graph shows how the overall mass changes as a reaction between marble chips and hydrochloric acid progresses. Describe how the graph shows the way the rate of reaction changes.

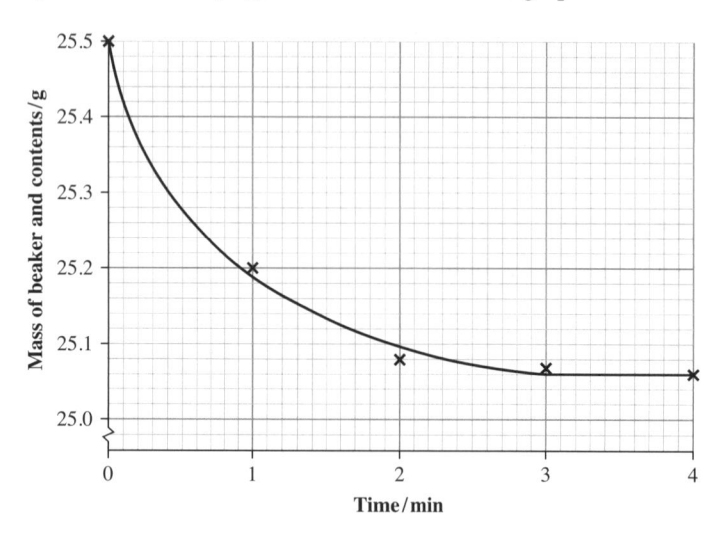

TIP
If you are asked when a reaction stops, find the point on the graph where the curve becomes horizontal. This is where the gradient, and therefore the rate of reaction, is zero. Then read this time from the scale.

....
....
....
....
....

Maths skill 3: Calculating the gradient of a straight-line graph

How does calculating the gradient of a straight-line graph help to calculate a physical property?

The density of a substance is equal to the mass of a sample divided by its volume:

$$\text{density} = \frac{\text{mass}}{\text{volume}}$$

The gradient of a graph is equal to the vertical change divided by the horizontal change.

This is the same as the change in vertical values divided by the change in horizontal values.

$$\text{gradient} = \frac{\text{vertical change}}{\text{horizontal change}} = \frac{\text{change in vertical values}}{\text{change in horizontal values}}$$

The gradient of a graph of mass (vertical axis) against volume (horizontal axis) is equal to the density.

$$\text{gradient} = \frac{\text{change in mass}}{\text{change in volume}} = \text{density}$$

TIP
It is important to learn what the gradient of certain graphs drawn in chemistry actually represents in real life.

Plotting several experimental measures on a graph and drawing a best-fit line should mean that your calculated density is closer to the true value than if you used an individual pair of measurements.

WORKED EXAMPLE 7

This graph shows the mass of lead plotted against the volume of lead. Calculate the gradient of the best-fit line on this graph, to find the density of lead.

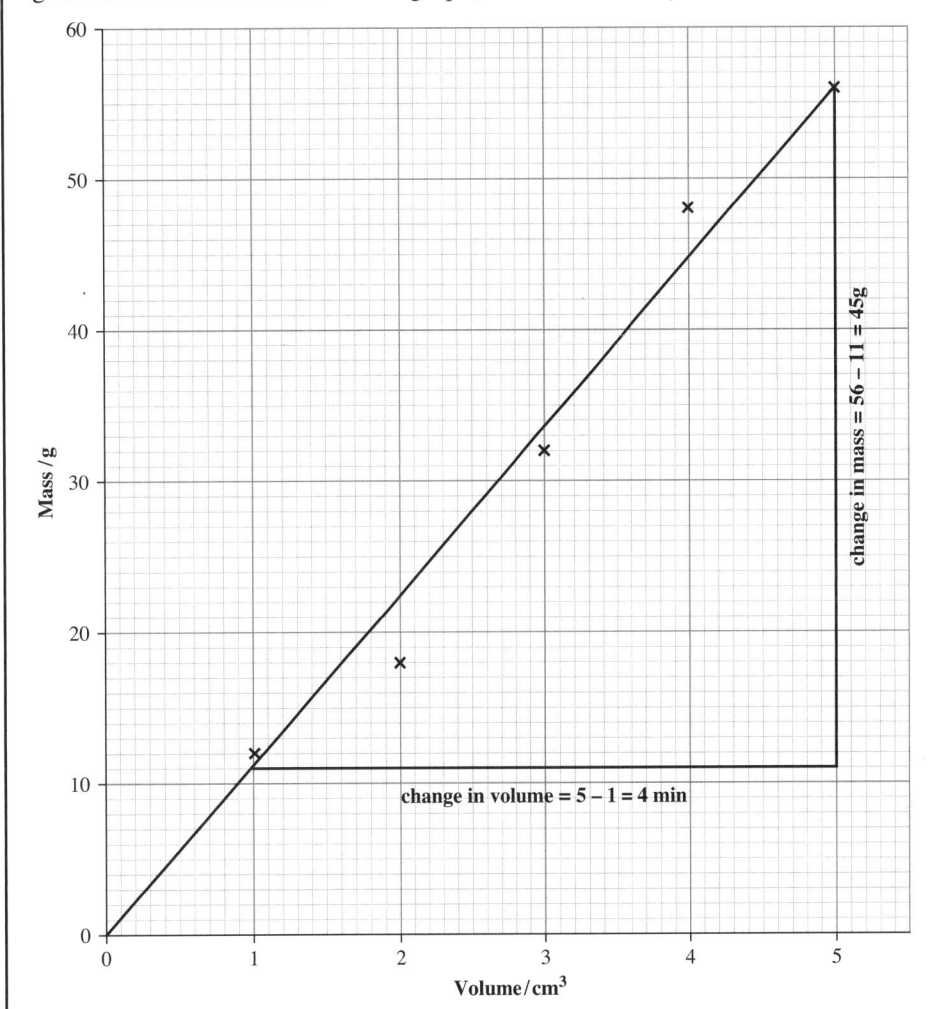

[Graph: Mass/g vs Volume/cm³, showing best-fit line with right-angled triangle. Labels: change in mass = 56 − 11 = 45 g; change in volume = 5 − 1 = 4 min]

Step 1 Select two clear points along the line.

Ensure that the distance between the points is at least half the length of the full line.

The first point is at 1 cm³ and 11 g.

The second point is at 5 cm³ and 56 g.

Step 2 Draw a right-angled triangle in which the line between these points forms the hypotenuse (the side opposite the right angle).

See graph.

Step 3 Use the triangle to calculate the gradient:

$$\text{gradient} = \frac{\text{vertical change}}{\text{horizontal change}} = \frac{\text{change in mass}}{\text{change in volume}}$$

$$= \frac{56 - 11}{5 - 1} = \frac{45}{4}$$

$$= 11.3$$

Remember to add in the correct units.

11.3 g/cm³

This is equal to the density of lead, which can be checked by referring to a data table.

> **TIP**
> The units for the gradient should be based on the units for mass divided by the units for volume.

Practice question 7

Calculate the gradient of the best-fit line on this graph, to find the density of copper.

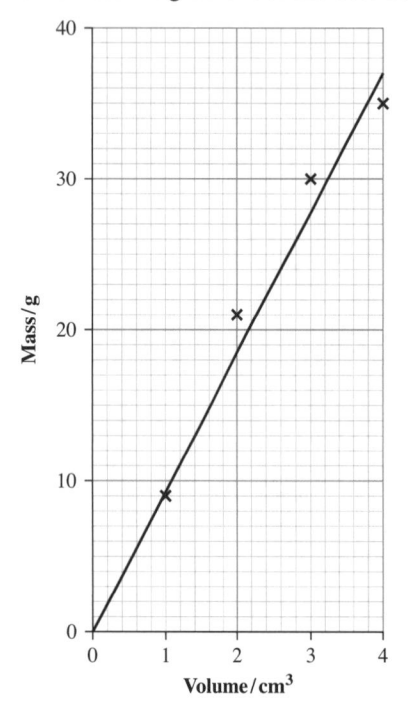

....

....

....

Practice question 8

Use this graph to calculate the density of iron.

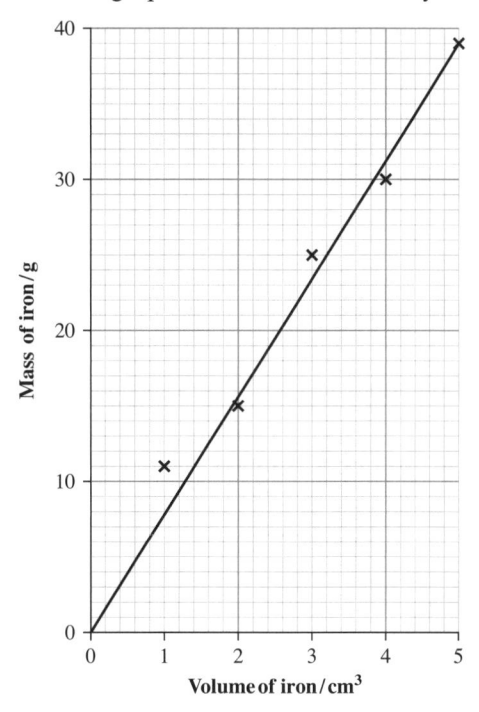

....
....
....

Further questions

1 The bar chart shows the melting points of the Group 1 elements.

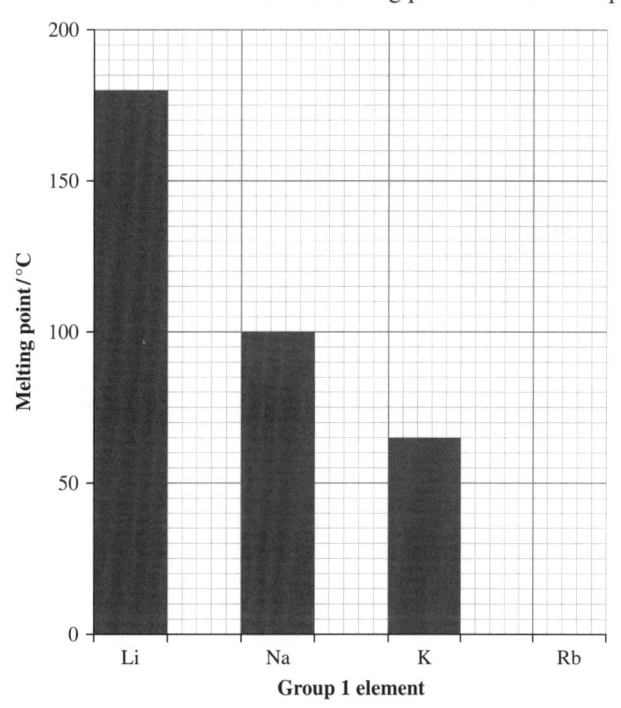

a i From the graph find the melting point of lithium (Li) to the nearest 5 °C.

....

ii Calculate the difference in melting points between lithium and potassium (K).

....

b i Describe the pattern shown by the graph.

....

ii Use the pattern to estimate the melting point of rubidium (Rb).

....

c If cut, lithium and sodium do not stay shiny for long. This is because they react with oxygen in the air to form lithium oxide and sodium oxide.

The pie charts below show the percentages (by mass) of lithium in lithium oxide and sodium in sodium oxide.

i Use the pie chart below to estimate the percentage (by mass) of lithium in lithium oxide.

....

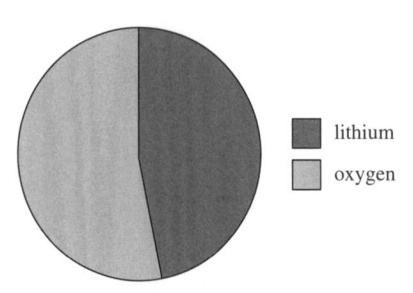

ii Use the pie chart below to estimate the percentage (by mass) of sodium in sodium oxide.

....

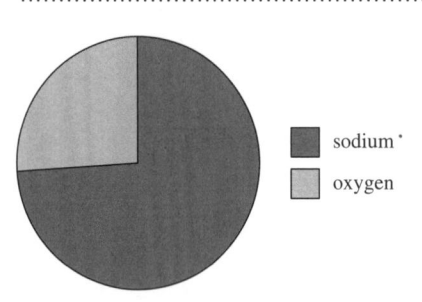

2 The graph below shows the maximum mass of sodium nitrate that dissolves in 100 g of water at different temperatures. This is called its solubility.

   a i Interpolate the graph to find the solubility of sodium nitrate at a temperature of 15 °C.

      ....

      ii Extrapolate the graph to find the solubility of sodium nitrate at 60 °C.

      ....

   b 50 g of sodium nitrate is added to 100 g of water and the water is then gradually warmed.

      Use the graph to find the temperature at which the sodium nitrate was fully dissolved.

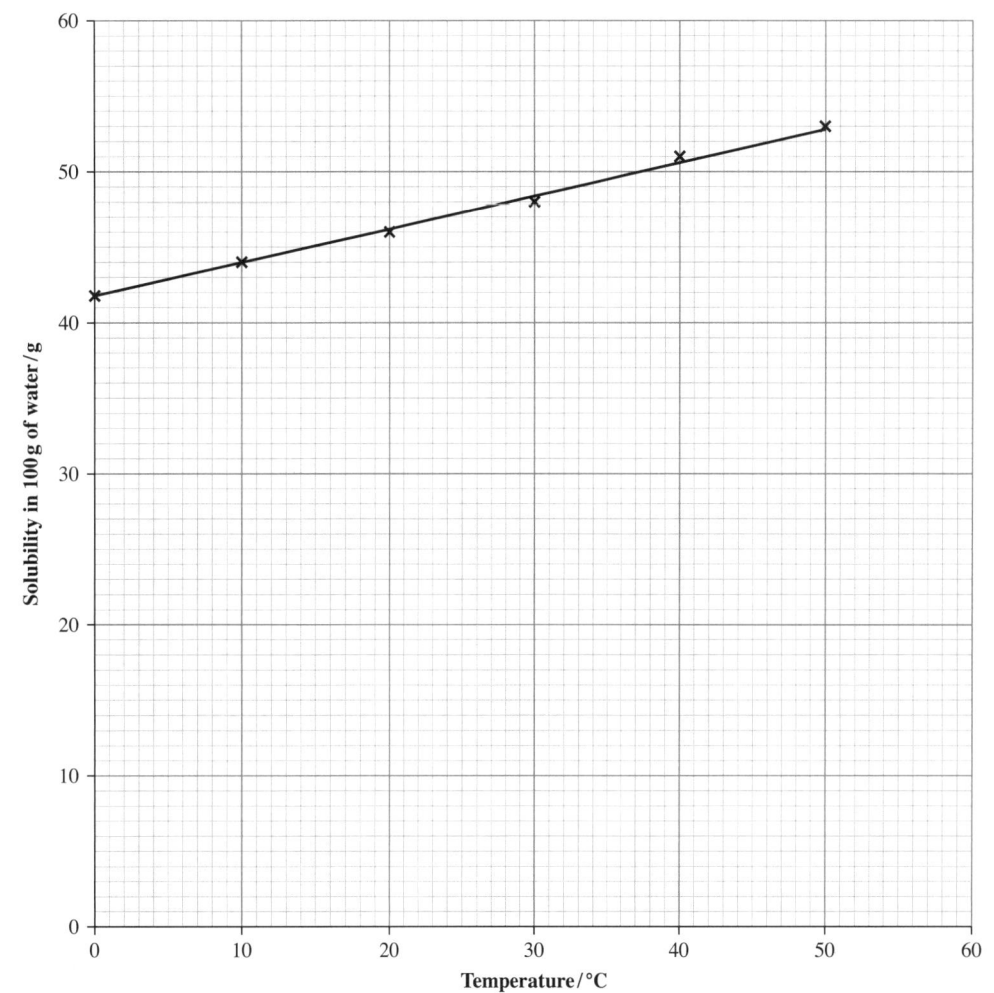

      ....

3 Hydrogen peroxide decomposes (breaks down) to form water and oxygen. A catalyst increases the rate of this reaction.

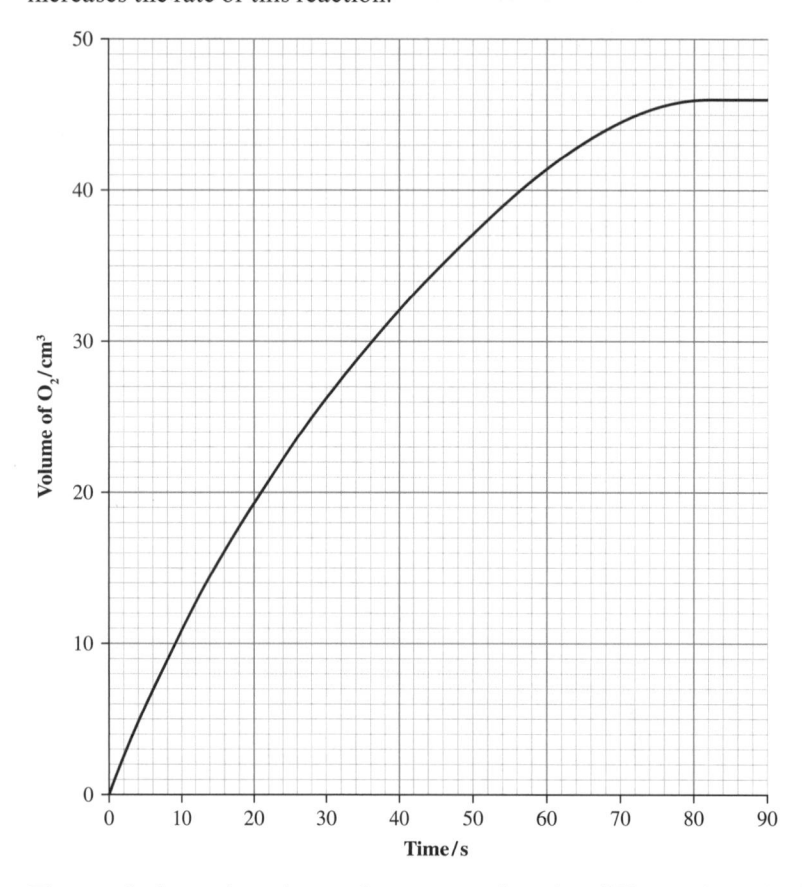

The graph shows the volume of oxygen produced at different times during a reaction.

a Describe the relationship between the volume of oxygen produced and time.

....

....

b The gradient of the graph shows the rate of reaction.

   i Use this to work out the units of the rate of reaction.

   ....

   ....

   ii Describe how the rate of reaction changes during the reaction.

   ....

   ....

c Use the graph to find:

   i the volume of oxygen produced after 30 seconds ....

   ii the final volume of oxygen produced ....

   iii the time taken for the reaction to finish. ....

Doing calculations

Why do you need to do calculations in chemistry?

You can find out lots of information about a chemical reaction by making observations. However, visual observations are *qualitative*. This means that they do not give you any numerical information about a reaction.

Calculations are used in *quantitative* chemistry to work out numerical information about a reaction, for example, the mass of a product that will be made or the mass of reactants needed to make a particular quantity of a product. Some calculations use data from the Periodic Table.

Other calculations use mathematical formulae that link different variables used in chemistry.

Maths focus 1: Using basic maths operations in calculations

Many calculations in chemistry can be carried out using the four basic maths operations: addition, subtraction, multiplication and division.

The challenge when answering a chemistry question is:

- first to write the correct calculation to find the answer
- then to carry out the calculation in the correct order.

Often, you will need to look up the values that are needed for the calculation in the Periodic Table. This means that you need to be able to combine your understanding of chemistry with your mathematical skills.

For example, if you want to work out the number of neutrons in an atom of lithium you first need to understand how to calculate the number of neutrons. This requires understanding of chemistry.

number of neutrons = nucleon (mass number) − atomic number

Then you need to look up the values in the Periodic Table.

Nucleon (mass) number of lithium = 7

Atomic number of lithium = 3

Finally, you substitute these values into your calculation.

Number of neutrons = 7 − 3 = 4

This last stage requires maths skills. This calculation was very simple but many chemical calculations use more than one maths operation, often involving brackets, so it is very important to remember the correct order in which operations and brackets should be carried out.

Cambridge IGCSE Chemistry Maths Skills

What maths skills do you need to calculate using basic mathematical operations?

> **TIP**
> Use **BIDMAS** to help remember the correct order of mathematical operations:
> **B**rackets, **I**ndices (powers), **D**ivision, **M**ultiplication, **A**ddition, **S**ubtraction

1	Working out the correct calculation	• Write down the calculation in terms of the elements, compounds, atoms or molecules involved • Look up the values needed for the calculation • Substitute the values into your planned calculation • Remember to use brackets if necessary

2	Using the operations in the correct order to calculate the answer	• Use **BIDMAS** to help remember the correct order of mathematical operations:
		  – complete calculations in brackets
		  – carry out any multiplication or division
		  – complete any addition or subtraction

Maths skills practice

How does using basic mathematical operations in calculations help to find the relative formula mass of a compound?

The relative formula mass (M_r) of a compound is the sum of the relative atomic masses (A_r) of the atoms shown in one formula unit of the compound.

To calculate relative formula mass it is important that you understand what the letters and numbers mean in a chemical formula.

The letters show the element symbol for each type of atom that makes up the compound. Each new symbol starts with a capital letter.

The small numbers (subscripts) tell you how many of that type of atom there are in each formula unit of the compound (see Figure 5.1).

Element symbol → Ca Cl$_2$ ← Element symbol
1 is never written   Subscript number

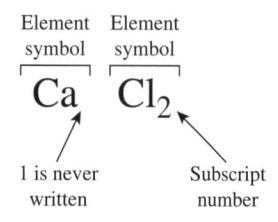

Figure 5.1 The use of subscripts in a chemical formula

Before you work on your maths skills, check that you understand chemical formulae correctly. Cover up the right-hand column in Table 5.1 and test yourself.

> **TIP**
> Remember that where there are brackets in a chemical formula the number of all atoms (ions) shown inside the brackets are multiplied by the small number outside the brackets.

Chemical formula	Atoms (or ions)
HCl	$1 \times H, 1 \times Cl$
CO_2	$1 \times C, 2 \times O$
H_2SO_4	$2 \times H, 1 \times S, 4 \times O$
$Mg(OH)_2$	$1 \times Mg, 2 \times O, 2 \times H$

Table 5.1 Some chemical formulae

Chapter 5: Doing calculations

Maths skill 1: Working out the correct calculation

WATCH OUT
Relative atomic mass and relative formula mass compare masses and have no units. They give the mass relative to a carbon-12 atom.

TIP
Remember to use brackets where necessary.

WORKED EXAMPLE 1

Write down the calculation required to find the relative formula mass (M_r) of calcium hydroxide.

The chemical formula for calcium hydroxide is $Ca(OH)_2$.

Step 1 Write down the calculation in terms of the elements, compound, atoms or ions involved.

You need to understand the chemistry in order to write the calculation.

M_r is calculated from relative atomic masses (A_r).

You need to use the chemical formula of the compound to work it out.

M_r of $Ca(OH)_2 = A_r$ of $Ca + (A_r$ of $O + A_r$ of $H) \times 2$
where A_r is relative atomic mass.

Step 2 Look up the values needed for the calculation.

These values may be provided in the questions or you may need to look them up in the Periodic Table.

A_r of $Ca = 40$ A_r of $O = 16$ A_r of $H = 1$

Step 3 Substitute the values into your planned calculation.

M_r of $Ca(OH)_2 = 40 + (16 + 1) \times 2$

Practice question 1

For each compound, write down the correct calculation for the relative formula mass.

a $Ca(OH)_2$

....

b $CaCO_3$

....

c HNO_3

....

d $MgSO_4$

....

e $KMnO_4$

....

f $Mg(NO_3)_2$

....

g $(NH_4)_2SO_4$

....

Maths skill 2: Using the operations in the correct order to calculate the answer

WORKED EXAMPLE 2

Calculate M_r of $Ca(OH)_2$

M_r of $Ca(OH)_2 = 40 + (16 + 1) \times 2$

Now follow the rules of BIDMAS.

Step 1 Complete any calculations in brackets.

M_r of $Ca(OH)_2 = 40 + (16 + 1) \times 2$

$= 40 + 17 \times 2$

Step 2 Carry out any multiplication or division.

$= 40 + 34$

Step 3 Complete any addition or subtraction.

$= 74$

Practice question 2

For each compound, calculate the relative formula mass. Make sure that you carry out the operations in the correct order. (You may use the calculations that you completed in Practice question 1.)

a $Ca(OH)_2$

....

b $CaCO_3$

....

c HNO_3

....

d $MgSO_4$

....

e $KMnO_4$

....

f $Mg(NO_3)_2$

....

g $(NH_4)_2SO_4$

....

TIP

Inside brackets, operations must still be used in the correct order so multiplication and division must come before addition and subtraction.

Maths focus 2: Calculating percentages

Percentages are commonly used in everyday life. If you take a test you may be given your result as a percentage.

'Per cent' means 'out of 100', so a score of 90% means that you got $\frac{90}{100}$ marks.

You can still get a percentage score for a test even if the test does not contain exactly 100 marks.

For example, a class is set a chemistry test where the maximum mark is 25.

To find the percentage for each student the teacher must first divide their score by 25 to find out what fraction of the available marks they earned.

Then, to find the percentage, she must multiply the fraction by 100.

Name	Score	Score/25	Percentage
Yeasmin	24	$\frac{24}{25}$	96%
Brandon	23	$\frac{23}{25}$	92%

Divide score by total score → Multiply fraction by 100

What maths skills do you need to calculate percentages?

1	Using available values to calculate the percentage	• Write down the percentage calculation • Look up the values needed for the calculation and find the totals • Calculate the percentage, using the operations in the correct order.

Maths skills practice

How does calculating percentages help you to compare the proportion of atoms of each element in a compound?

A chemical formula shows the relative number of atoms in one formula unit of the compound.

For example, in water (H_2O), for every 2 hydrogen atoms there is 1 oxygen atom. In terms of the number of atoms, oxygen makes up a third of the compound.

However, the atoms have very different relative atomic masses. The relative atomic mass of hydrogen is only 1. The relative atomic mass of oxygen is 16 times greater, so the percentage by mass of oxygen in water is very different. It is 89% (to two significant figures).

Cambridge IGCSE Chemistry Maths Skills

WORKED EXAMPLE 3

Calculate the percentage by mass of oxygen in water.

Step 1 Write down the percentage calculation.

$$\text{percentage by mass of oxygen in water} = \frac{\text{total mass of oxygen}}{M_r \text{ water}} \times 100$$

Step 2 Look up the values needed for the calculation and find the totals.

To find the percentage mass you need to know the A_r of each element in the compound.

$$A_r: H = 1.0 \qquad A_r: O = 16$$

The chemical formula shows only one O atom, so the total mass of the element is the same as its relative atomic mass (16).

The total mass of the compound equals the M_r of H_2O which is: $2 \times 1 + 16 = 18$

Step 3 Calculate the percentage, using the operations in the correct order.

KEY QUESTIONS TO ASK YOURSELF:

- How can I write out the calculation to make it easier?

  The way you write out the calculation can make it easier to calculate correctly. If you write $16 \div 18 \times 100$ you need to remember to use BIDMAS and work from left to right, but writing the calculation in the form $\frac{16}{18} \times 100$ makes the order of calculation much clearer.

  $$\frac{16}{18} \times 100 = 88.88$$

- To how many significant figures should I record the answer?

  Relative atomic mass in your Periodic Table is given to two significant figures, so the percentage by mass should not be written to more significant figures than this.

  This is 89% to two significant figures.

LINK
See Maths focus 1, 'Using basic maths operations in calculations'

LINK
See Chapter 1, Maths focus 3, Maths skill 2, 'Writing numbers to the required number of significant figures (sf)'

WATCH OUT
To find the percentage by mass of hydrogen in water, first find the mass of hydrogen atoms (H) in the compound (1.0 + 1.0 = 2) then divide by the relative molecular mass (M_r) of the compound.
$\frac{2}{18} \times 100 = 11\%$
to two significant figures

Practice question 3

For each element, calculate the percentage by mass of calcium carbonate.

The chemical formula of calcium carbonate is $CaCO_3$.

a Ca

....

b C

....

c O

....

Practice question 4

Calculate the percentage by mass of:

a N in HNO_3

....

b Mg in $MgSO_4$

....

c Mg in $Mg(NO_3)_2$

....

d N in $(NH_4)_2SO_4$

....

....

Maths focus 3: Using mathematical formulae in calculations (Supplement)

A mathematical **equation**, such as $y = \frac{z}{x}$, shows the relationship between variables. It allows you to use the values of two or more variables to calculate an unknown variable.

What happens if you know the variable on the left-hand side but you do not know one of the variables on the right-hand side? You need to rearrange the equation so that the variable you want to find is on the left-hand side.

An equation remains true, provided that the same mathematical action is applied to both sides.

When you are manipulating or rearranging a mathematical equation, you can use the fact that $\frac{x}{x} = 1$ to cancel some variables. Suppose that the unknown variable was z.

$$y = \frac{z}{x}$$

Multiplying both sides by x gives: $xy = \frac{xz}{x}$

The xs on the right-hand side cancel, leaving $xy = z$

Then all you have to do is to swap sides to give $z = xy$.

A mathematical equation that shows the relationship between physical quantities is called a **formula**.

This method or rearranging will work with a mathematical formula of the same form as the mathematical equation $y = \frac{z}{x}$, for example:

$$\text{number of moles} = \frac{\text{mass}}{\text{molar mass}}$$

Cambridge IGCSE Chemistry Maths Skills

What maths skills do you need to use mathematical formulae in calculations?

1	Substituting values into a mathematical formula	• List the variables and select the correct mathematical formula to calculate the unknown
		• Write down the values of the known variables and their units
		• Substitute the values and units into the mathematical formula and calculate the unknown.
2	Rearranging a mathematical formula	• Write down the mathematical formula and decide if it is in the form $z = xy$ or $y = \frac{z}{x}$
		• Identify which variable you are trying to find, and rearrange the mathematical formula to put it on the left-hand side
		• Substitute the values and units and calculate the unknown
3	Carrying out a multi-step calculation using two mathematical formulae	• Select the correct mathematical formula to calculate the unknown, rearrange if necessary
		• Substitute values and identify any further unknowns.
		• Select a mathematical formula that could let you calculate this unknown
		• Substitute values into the second formula and calculate
		• Put the calculated value back into the first formula

> **WATCH OUT**
>
> number of moles $= \dfrac{\text{mass}}{\text{molar mass}}$
>
> Make sure the mass is in grams (g) and the molar mass is in grams per mole (g/mol).

> **WATCH OUT**
>
> number of moles $= \dfrac{\text{volume}}{\text{molar volume}}$
>
> Make sure the volume is in cubic decimetres (dm^3).
> $1\,dm^3 = 1000\,cm^3$ so to convert from cm^3 into dm^3 divide by 1000.

> **WATCH OUT**
>
> concentration $= \dfrac{\text{number of moles}}{\text{volume}}$
>
> Make sure that the volume is in cubic decimetres (dm^3) and the concentration is in moles/dm^3.

Maths skills practice

How does using a mathematical formula in calculations help you to find out about the amount of a substance?

If you weigh out the relative atomic mass of an element, in grams, it will contain 6.02×10^{23} atoms.

This very large number is known as *Avogadro's constant* and represents 1 mole of the element.

Similarly, the relative formula mass of a compound in grams contains 1 mole of formula units (or molecules).

The mass of 1 mole is known as the *molar mass* and has units of grams per mole (g/mol).

Mathematical formulae are very useful when calculating the amount of a substance. If you already know the number of moles, you can rearrange the mathematical formulae to find other quantities such as volume or mass.

The formula number of moles $= \dfrac{\text{mass}}{\text{molar mass}}$ allows you to calculate the number of moles in a given mass of a compound.

The formula number of moles $= \dfrac{\text{volume}}{\text{molar volume}}$ allows to you calculate the number of moles in a given volume of a gas.

The formula concentration $= \dfrac{\text{number of moles}}{\text{volume}}$ allows you to calculate the concentration of a solution.

Chapter 5: Doing calculations

Maths skill 1: Substituting values into a mathematical formula

WORKED EXAMPLE 4

How many moles of calcium carbonate are there in 0.3 kg of calcium carbonate?

The molar mass of calcium carbonate is 100 g.

Step 1 List the variables and select the correct mathematical formula to calculate the unknown.

Your list of variables should also include the unknown.

The variables in the question are mass in grams and molar mass in g/mol. The unknown is the number of moles.

Select the correct mathematical formula to calculate the unknown.

$$\text{number of moles} = \frac{\text{mass}}{M_r}$$

Step 2 Write down the values of the known variables and their units.

Remember to convert any inconsistent units.

Mass has been given as 0.3 kg.

Multiply by 1000 to convert kg to g (300 g).

Step 3 Substitute the values and units into the mathematical formula and calculate the unknown.

$$\text{number of moles} = \frac{300\,\text{g}}{100\,\text{g/mol}}$$

$$= 3\,\text{mol}$$

> **TIP**
>
> If you are not given the M_r, remember that you can calculate it from the chemical formula and the relative atomic masses which you can find in the Periodic Table.

Practice question 5

How many moles of each compound are there in:

a 10 g of magnesium oxide (MgO)

....

b 285 g of magnesium chloride ($MgCl_2$)

....

c 10 g of calcium carbonate ($CaCO_3$)

....

d 34 g of ammonia (NH_3)

....

e 1.8 kg of water (H_2O)?

....

Practice question 6

The molar volume of a gas is 24 dm³. How many moles are there in:

a 36 dm³ of oxygen

....

b 3 dm³ of carbon dioxide

....

c 12 dm³ of nitrogen

....

d 6000 cm³ of helium

....

e 300 cm³ of oxygen?

....

Practice question 7

What is the concentration of:

a 0.5 moles of hydrogen chloride (HCl) in a final volume of 1 dm³

....

b 0.5 moles of sodium hydroxide (NaOH) in a final volume of 0.5 dm³

....

c 1 mole of hydrogen chloride (HCl) in a final volume of 2 dm³

....

d 0.5 moles of potassium hydroxide (KOH) in a final volume of 500 cm³

....

e 0.5 moles of sulfuric acid (H₂SO₄) in a final volume of 250 cm³?

....

Chapter 5: Doing calculations

Maths skill 2: Rearranging a mathematical formula

You can use the methods in Table 5.2 to rearrange mathematical formulae to find any one of the three variables.

Mathematical formula	What do you want to find? (the unknown variable)	How to do it
$y = xz$	y	Multiply z by x
$y = xz$	z (one of the two numbers multiplied together)	Swap sides to get $xz = y$. Then divide both sides by x (as it is the other part of xz) to get $z = \dfrac{y}{x}$.
$y = \dfrac{z}{x}$	y	Divide z by x.
$y = \dfrac{z}{x}$	z	Multiply both sides by x to get $xy = z$. Swap sides to get $z = xy$.
$y = \dfrac{z}{x}$	x	Multiply both sides by x to get $xy = z$. Then divide both sides by y to get $x = \dfrac{z}{y}$.

Table 5.2 Methods to rearrange mathematical formulae

WORKED EXAMPLE 5

What is the volume of 0.25 moles of carbon dioxide?

molar volume = $24\,dm^3/mol$

Step 1 Write down the mathematical formula and decide if it is in the form $y = xz$ or $y = \dfrac{z}{x}$.

The formula is: number of moles = $\dfrac{\text{volume}}{\text{molar volume}}$

This has the form $y = \dfrac{z}{x}$.

Step 2 Identify which variable you are trying to find and rearrange the mathematical formula to put it on the left-hand side.

moles = $\dfrac{\boxed{\text{volume}}}{\text{molar volume}}$ $\qquad$ $y = \dfrac{\boxed{z}}{x}$

Multiply both sides by x to get $xy = z$

Swap sides: $\qquad\qquad\qquad z = xy$

volume = moles × molar volume

Step 3 Substitute the values and units and calculate the unknown.

volume = 0.25 moles × $24\,dm^3$/moles

= $6\,dm^3$

Cambridge IGCSE Chemistry Maths Skills

Practice question 8

Useful mathematical formulae

$$\text{number of moles} = \frac{\text{mass}}{\text{molar mass } M_r}$$

$$\text{number of moles} = \frac{\text{volume (in dm}^3\text{)}}{\text{molar volume (24 dm}^3\text{)}}$$

$$\text{concentration} = \frac{\text{number of moles}}{\text{volume (in dm}^3\text{)}}$$

Rearrange the appropriate mathematical formulae from the box above to calculate:

a the volume of 2 moles of carbon dioxide (molar volume is 24 dm^3)

....

b the mass of 0.5 moles of calcium carbonate (CaCO$_3$)

....

c the number of moles of sodium hydroxide (NaOH) in 0.25 dm^3 of a solution with concentration 0.1 mol/dm^3

....

d the volume of solution with concentration 0.5 mol/dm^3 that contains 0.04 moles of sodium hydroxide (NaOH).

....

Practice question 9

a Given that 36 g of water (H$_2$O) contains 2 moles of water, show that the M_r of water is 18.

....

b Given that 2 moles of helium occupy 48 dm^3, show that the molar gas volume is 24 dm^3.

....

Maths skill 3: Carrying out a multi-step calculation using two mathematical formulae

TIP
Some chemistry questions refer to more than one substance, so it is helpful to record a variable as concentration of NaOH or volume of HCl in order to keep track of what the values mean.

WORKED EXAMPLE 6

Calculate the concentration of a solution of sodium hydroxide (NaOH) that contains 5 g of NaOH in a final volume of 250 cm^3.

Step 1 Select the correct mathematical formula to calculate the unknown (rearrange if necessary).

The variables (including any unknowns) in the question are

concentration of NaOH (unknown)

mass of NaOH = 5 g

volume of solution = 250 cm^3 or 0.25 dm^3

Therefore a suitable mathematical formulae to calculate the unknown is

$$\text{concentration of NaOH} = \frac{\text{number of moles of NaOH}}{\text{volume in dm}^3}$$

Step 2 Substitute values and identify any further unknowns.

$$\text{concentration of NaOH} = \frac{\text{number of moles of NaOH}}{0.25}$$

Number of moles of NaOH is still unknown.

Step 3 Select a mathematical formula that could let you calculate this unknown.

$$\text{number of moles of NaOH} = \frac{\text{mass of NaOH}}{M_r \text{ of NaOH}}$$

Step 4 Substitute values into the second formula and calculate the additional unknown.

$$\text{number of moles of NaOH} = \frac{5}{40} = 0.125 \text{ moles}$$

Step 5 Put the calculated value back into the first formula.

$$\text{concentration of NaOH} = \frac{\text{number of moles of NaOH}}{0.25} = \frac{0.125}{0.25}$$
$$= 0.5 \text{ mol/dm}^3$$

Practice question 10

Calculate the mass of sodium hydroxide (NaOH) needed to make a volume of 0.02 dm^3 of solution with concentration 0.2 mol/dm^3. M_r of NaOH = 40

....
....
....
....
....
....
....
....
....
....
....
....
....
....

Cambridge IGCSE Chemistry Maths Skills

> **TIP**
> Remember that the M_r of a compound can be calculated from its chemical formula and data from the Periodic Table.

Practice question 11

A reaction produces 0.6 g of carbon dioxide. Calculate the volume of gas produced.

....

....

....

....

....

....

....

....

....

....

....

....

....

Maths focus 4: Calculating using ratios

A ratio shows the size or quantity, a, of one thing compared to the size or quantity, b, of another thing. It is written in the form $a:b$.

In Figure 5.2 the ratio of apples to bananas is $1:2$. For every 1 apple there are 2 bananas.

Figure 5.2 A ratio of $1:2$

Figure 5.3 shows more fruit. The ratio this time is $3:6$. For every 3 apples there are 6 bananas.

Figure 5.3 A ratio of $3:6$

Ratios are usually written in their simplest form. If the numbers on both sides of a ratio are divided by the same number (a common factor) then the ratio is still true.

In this case, dividing both sides of the ratio $3:6$ by 3 gives a ratio of $1:2$. So the ratio in Figure 5.3 is equivalent to the one in Figure 5.2. For every 1 apple there are still 2 bananas.

Suppose you were asked to work out how many bananas there would be if there were 7 apples. This would be tricky to work out from the second ratio $3:6$. Simplifying the ratio to $1:2$ makes the calculation easier.

If both sides of a ratio are multiplied by the same number then the ratio remains true.

Chapter 5: Doing calculations

> **TIP**
> Remember that the number 1 is not written in chemical formulae or chemical equations.

> **TIP**
> In a balanced chemical equation the large numbers show the ratio in which substances react and are formed. This is called the stoichiometry of the equation.

> **TIP**
> In chemical formulae and balanced chemical equations the number 1 is not shown.

So to answer the problem, the ratio 1:2 needs to be multiplied on both sides by 7, giving 7:14. The answer is that if there are 7 apples there will be 14 bananas.

Ratios are very important in chemistry, as they are the basis for both chemical formulae and balanced chemical equations.

In a chemical formula the small numbers (subscripts) show the number of atoms (or ions) of each element in the formula unit of a compound.

Magnesium oxide (MgO) has a ratio of Mg ions : O ions of 1:1.

Magnesium chloride ($MgCl_2$) has a ratio of Mg ions : Cl ions of 1:2.

The large numbers in a chemical equation show the ratio of the substances reacting.

For example, the balanced chemical equation:

$$2Mg + O_2 \rightarrow 2MgO$$

This shows that magnesium reacts with oxygen molecules in a ratio of 2:1.

What maths skills do you need to calculate using ratios?

1	Using ratio to work out reacting masses	• Use the balanced chemical equation to write down the ratio of reactants to products
		• Use the ratio and relative formula masses to work out the reacting masses
		• Calculate the reacting mass required or formed by the given quantity of reactant or product
2	Using ratio and moles to work out reacting masses (*Supplement*)	• Use the balanced chemical equation to write down the ratio of reactants to products
		• Calculate the number of moles of reactant (or product) in the question
		• Use the ratio to work out the number of moles of product formed (or reactant required)
		• Convert the number of moles of product (or reactant) into a mass

Maths skills practice

How does using a ratio in calculations help you to work out chemical quantities?

In a balanced chemical equation the large numbers show the ratio in which elements and compounds react and are produced.

Using relative atomic mass and relative formula mass, it is possible to work out the mass of product produced by a given mass of reactant. You can also work out the reverse, the mass of reactant required to make a particular mass of product.

You can also calculate reacting masses using the mathematical formula:

$$\text{number of moles} = \frac{\text{mass}}{\text{molar mass}}$$

> **LINK**
> See Maths focus 2, 'Using percentages to calculate'.

In real life the actual amount of product (yield) may be lower than the calculated amount. The calculated mass of product is referred to as the theoretical yield:

$$\text{percentage yield} = \frac{\text{actual mass of product}}{\text{theoretical yield of product}} \times 100$$

Cambridge IGCSE Chemistry Maths Skills

Maths skill 1: Using ratio to work out reacting masses

WORKED EXAMPLE 7

What mass of carbon dioxide is produced by 30 g of carbon?

$$C + O_2 \rightarrow CO_2$$

Step 1 Use the balanced chemical equation to write down the ratio of reactants to products.

It may help to circle the reactant and product of interest in the question.

$$\text{\textcircled{C}} + O_2 \rightarrow \text{\textcircled{CO}}_2$$

The ratio $C : CO_2$ is $1 : 1$.

Step 2 Use the ratio and relative formula masses to work out the reacting masses.

Relative atomic mass of C is 12.

Relative formula mass of CO_2 is 44.

This means that 12 g of carbon reacts to produce 44 g of carbon dioxide.

Step 3 Calculate the reacting mass required or formed by the given quantity of reactant or product.

Divide by the relative atomic (or relative formula) mass of the reactant to convert the ratio to the form $1 : b$.

$\dfrac{12}{12}$ g of C produces $\dfrac{44}{12}$ g of CO_2

Multiply both sides by the mass of reactant in the question.

$\dfrac{12}{12} \times 30$ g of C produces $\dfrac{44}{12} \times 30$ g of CO_2.

So 30 g of C produces 110 g of CO_2.

> **TIP**
> The question does not ask about O_2, so this can be ignored.

> **TIP**
> To find the mass of product formed by a given mass of reactant:
> - divide by the mass of the reactant to convert the ratio to the form $1 : b$
> - multiply both sides by the mass of reactant in the question.

Practice question 12

When copper carbonate is heated it decomposes to form copper oxide and carbon dioxide.

$$CuCO_3 \rightarrow CuO + CO_2$$

a Calculate the relative formula masses of $CuCO_3$, CuO and CO_2.

....

b Calculate the mass of copper oxide formed from 31 g of $CuCO_3$.

....

....

....

c Calculate the mass of CO_2 formed from 31 g of $CuCO_3$.

....

> **TIP**
> Do not round the answer before the end, as this will change the final answer.

Chapter 5: Doing calculations

Practice question 13

Magnesium reacts with oxygen to form magnesium oxide.

$$2Mg + O_2 \rightarrow 2MgO$$

a What mass of magnesium oxide is produced by 0.96 g of magnesium?

....

....

....

b What mass of magnesium is required to produce 0.2 g of magnesium oxide?

....

....

....

....

> **TIP**
> To find the mass of reactant required to make a given quantity of product:
> - divide by the mass of the product to convert the ratio to the form $a:1$
> - multiply both sides by the mass of product in the question.

Practice question 14

Nitrogen reacts with hydrogen to produce ammonia.

$$N_2 + 3H_2 \rightarrow 2NH_3$$

a What mass of ammonia is produced by 0.7 g of nitrogen?

....

....

....

b What mass of hydrogen is required to produce 0.17 g of ammonia?

....

....

....

Maths skill 2: Using ratio and moles to work out reacting masses (Supplement)

> **WORKED EXAMPLE 8**
>
> What mass of carbon dioxide is produced by 30 g of carbon?
>
> $$C + O_2 \rightarrow CO_2$$
>
> **Step 1** Use the balanced chemical equation to find the ratio of reactants to products.
>
> $$\boxed{C} + O_2 \rightarrow \boxed{CO_2}$$
>
> The ratio $C:CO_2$ is $1:1$.
>
> This ratio tells you that 1 mole of carbon produces 1 mole of carbon dioxide.

Step 2 Calculate the number of moles of reactant (or product) in the question.

Use the formula number of moles = $\dfrac{\text{mass}}{\text{molar mass}}$ to work out the number of moles of reactant in the question.

number of moles of carbon = $\dfrac{\text{mass}}{\text{molar mass}} = \dfrac{30}{12}$

Step 3 Use the ratio to work out the number of moles of product formed (or reactant required).

The ratio is 1 : 1 so $\dfrac{30}{12}$ moles of carbon dioxide are produced.

Step 4 Convert the number of moles of product (or reactant) into a mass.

mass of CO_2 = number of moles CO_2 × molar mass of CO_2

$= \dfrac{30}{12} \times 44$

$= 110\,g$

Practice question 15

When copper carbonate is heated it decomposes to form copper oxide and carbon dioxide.

$$CuCO_3 \rightarrow CuO + CO_2$$

a Calculate the relative formula masses of $CuCO_3$, CuO and CO_2.

....

b Calculate the mass of copper oxide formed from 372 g of $CuCO_3$.

....
....
....
....

c Calculate the mass of CO_2 formed from 372 g of $CuCO_3$.

....
....
....

Practice question 16

Sulfur reacts with oxygen to form sulfur dioxide.

$$S + O_2 \rightarrow SO_2$$

a What mass of sulfur dioxide is produced by 3.2 g of sulfur?

....

....

....

....

b What mass of sulfur is required to produce 3.2 g of sulfur dioxide?

....

....

Practice question 17

Nitrogen reacts with hydrogen to produce ammonia.

$$N_2 + 3H_2 \rightarrow 2NH_3$$

a What mass of ammonia is produced by 21 g of nitrogen?

....

....

....

....

....

....

b What mass of hydrogen is required to produce 0.34 g of ammonia?

....

....

....

....

....

Further questions

1 Blue copper sulfate crystals are a hydrated form of copper sulfate. They contain water molecules. White anhydrous copper sulfate contains no water.

   a i Calculate the relative formula mass of anhydrous copper sulfate with chemical formula $CuSO_4$.

   ....

   ii Calculate the relative formula mass of hydrated copper sulfate with chemical formula $CuSO_4 \cdot 5H_2O$.

   ....

   b Calculate the percentage by mass of water in hydrated copper sulfate.

   ....

2 Nitrogen fertilisers are made up of compounds containing nitrogen. Nitrogen is important for plant growth.

   a Calculate the percentage by mass of nitrogen in each of these fertilisers.

   i ammonium nitrate, NH_4NO_3

   ....

   ....

   ii ammonium sulphate, $(NH_4)_2SO_4$

   ....

   ....

   iii urea, $CO(NH_2)_2$

   ....

   ....

   b Ammonium nitrate is produced by the reaction between ammonia and nitric acid.

   $$NH_3(g) + HNO_3(aq) \rightarrow NH_4NO_3(aq)$$

   Calculate the mass of ammonia required to produce 50 kg of ammonium nitrate.

   ....

   ....

   ....

   ....

   ....

3 A blast furnace is used to extract iron from iron oxide. (Supplement)

$$Fe_2O_3(s) + 3CO(g) \rightarrow 2Fe(s) + 3CO_2(g)$$

a Calculate the number of moles of iron oxide in 16 kg.

....

....

....

b i Use the chemical equation to work out how many moles of iron are produced by 16 kg of iron oxide.

....

ii Calculate the mass of iron produced.

....

c During the process carbon dioxide is produced as a waste product.

i Calculate the number of moles of carbon dioxide produced by 16 kg of iron oxide.

....

ii Calculate the volume of carbon dioxide produced (molar volume = 24 dm³).

....

....

....

....

4 A student pipettes 25 cm³ of 0.1 M of sodium hydroxide into a flask and adds indicator. (Supplement)

She adds hydrochloric acid from a burette until the indicator changes colour. She repeats this process three times.

The mean volume of hydrochloric acid that she adds is 15.6 cm³.

The chemical equation for the reaction is:

$$HCl(aq) + NaOH(aq) \rightarrow NaCl(aq) + H_2O(l)$$

a Calculate the number of moles of sodium hydroxide in the flask.

....

....

....

....

b Use the chemical equation to work out how many moles of hydrochloric acid the sodium hydroxide reacts with.

....

c Calculate the unknown concentration of hydrochloric acid in the burette.

....

....

....

....

Working with shape

Why do you need to work with shape in chemistry?

In chemistry you need to be able to understand and compare surface areas, or surface area to volume ratios of solid samples of a material. Usually this material will be an irregular shape, but learning about regular 3D shapes is a good way to improve your understanding of these ideas.

Maths focus 1: Comparing surface area and volume

The **surface area** of a solid is the total area of its surfaces. You can calculate the surface area of a geometrically regular shape by adding the areas of all its faces.

The surface area of a solid increases if the solid is broken up, as more surface is exposed.

The surface area : volume ratio is a useful way to compare the amount of exposed surface for each unit of volume. It is important that the surface area and volume are given in the same basic unit. Unlike ratios in maths, the surface area : volume ratio does have a unit. For example the ratio of $cm^2 : cm^3$ has units of /cm (per centimetre).

What maths skills do you need to be able to compare surface area and volume?

1	Calculating surface area	• For an individual regular 3D shape:
		  – count the faces of each shape
		  – calculate the area of each face
		  – calculate the total area of all faces
		• If a shape is cut into smaller shapes, find the total surface area of all the shapes

2	Comparing the surface area to volume ratio	• Calculate the total surface area • Calculate the total volume • Write the full surface area : volume ratio • Write the surface area : volume ratio as a single number

Maths skills practice

How does comparing surface area and volume help to explain differences in rates of reaction?

Many chemical reactions involve a solid reactant. Only the particles on the outside of the solid come into contact with the other reactant(s), therefore the greater the surface area, the faster the rate of reaction.

For example, when reacting marble chips and then the same mass of powdered marble with hydrochloric acid, the same mass (and therefore the same volume) of marble has very different surface areas.

You can say that the powdered marble has a higher surface area : volume ratio because the exposed surface area is greater for the powdered marble than for the marble chips, for each unit of volume.

Chapter 6: Working with shape

Figure 6.1 The rate of reaction of 1 g of marble powder (in the left-hand beaker) with hydrochloric acid is much faster than with 1 g of marble chips (in the right-hand beaker)

Maths skill 1: Calculating surface area

TIP
Remember that units of area are squared units.

LINK
See Chapter 1, Maths focus 1, Maths skills 2 'Writing the unit symbol'.

WORKED EXAMPLE 1

Calculate the surface area of a cubic sodium chloride crystal with sides of length 2 mm (see Figure 6.2).

Figure 6.2 A sodium chloride crystal

Step 1 Count the faces.

Since the crystal is a cube it has 6 square faces.

Step 2 Calculate the area of each face.

Each face is a square of side 2 mm. The area of each square face is $2 \times 2 = 4 \, mm^2$

Step 3 Calculate the total area of all faces.

Total area = 6 × area of square face
= 6 × 4
= 24 mm^2

Cambridge IGCSE Chemistry Maths Skills

Practice question 1

Calculate the surface area of a cubic crystal of iron sulfide with sides of length 3 mm.

....

....

....

Practice question 2

Calculate the surface area of an octahedral diamond crystal.

Each face has an area of 4 mm².

Figure 6.3 An octahedral diamond

....

....

....

Practice question 3

Calculate the surface area of a cylinder of chalk with diameter 0.5 cm and length 10 cm.

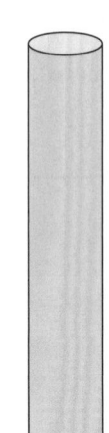

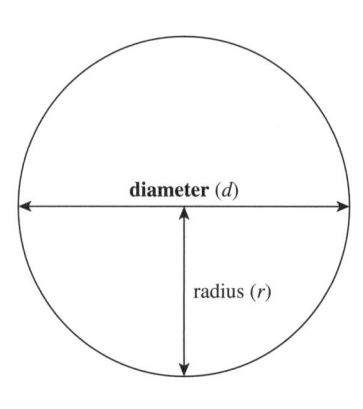

TIP
To calculate the area of the circular face use πr^2 (where r is the radius). The value of π (pi) may be found by using the π key on a calculator.

Chapter 6: Working with shape

> **TIP**
> To calculate the area of the curved face, imagine unwrapping it to make a rectangle so the area is equal to
>
> length of the cylinder × circumference of the circular face

The **circumference** is the length of the perimeter of the circle and is equal to πd or $2\pi r$.

....

....

....

....

....

Practice question 4

A cube-shaped block of aluminium measures $1\,cm \times 1\,cm \times 1\,cm$.

a Calculate the surface area of the block.

....

....

b The block is then cut into 8 equally sized cubes each measuring $0.5\,cm \times 0.5\,cm \times 0.5\,cm$.

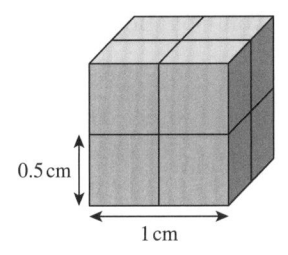

Calculate the new surface area.

....

....

Maths skill 2: Comparing the surface area to volume ratio

WORKED EXAMPLE 2

Compare the surface area : volume ratio of a $2\,cm \times 2\,cm \times 2\,cm$ cube with the surface area : volume ratio when it is broken up into eight $1\,cm \times 1\,cm \times 1\,cm$ cubes.

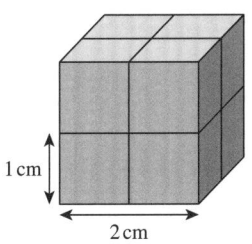

Consider the $2\,cm \times 2\,cm \times 2\,cm$ cube.

The $2\,cm \times 2\,cm \times 2\,cm$ cube:

Step 1 Calculate the total surface area.

$$\text{Surface area} = 6 \times 2 \times 2$$
$$= 24\,cm^2$$

> **TIP**
> The volume of a cube is equal to its length cubed.

Cambridge IGCSE Chemistry Maths Skills

> **TIP**
> Remember that units of volume are cubed units.

> **LINK**
> See Chapter 1, Maths focus 1, Maths skills 2 'Writing the unit symbol'.

> **WATCH OUT**
> The base unit for the volume should be the same as for the surface area to make the ratio valid. For example, if surface area is in m^2 then the volume should be in m^3.

Step 2 Calculate the total volume.

$$\text{Volume} = 2^3 = 8\,cm^3$$

Step 3 Write the full surface area : volume ratio.

24 : 8

Step 4 Write the surface area : volume ratio as a single number with a unit.

$$\frac{24\,cm^2}{8\,cm^3} = 3/cm$$

The eight 1 cm × 1 cm × 1 cm cubes:

Step 1 Calculate the total surface area.

$$\text{Total surface area} = 8 \times 6 \times 1$$
$$= 48\,cm^2$$

Step 2 Calculate the total volume.

$$\text{Total volume} = 8 \times 1^3$$
$$= 8\,cm^3$$

Step 3 Write the full surface area : volume ratio.

48 : 8

Step 4 Write the surface area : volume ratio as a single number.

$$\frac{48\,cm^2}{8\,cm^3} = 6/cm$$

Breaking the cube apart has increased the surface area : volume ratio from 3/cm to 6/cm.

Practice question 5

Compare the surface area : volume ratio of a 3 cm × 3 cm × 3 cm cube with the surface area : volume ratio when it is broken into separate 1 cm × 1 cm × 1 cm cubes.

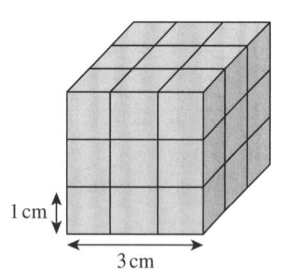

....
....
....
....
....
....

Practice question 6

a   Work out the surface area : volume ratio of:

   i   one 4 cm × 4 cm × 4 cm cube

   ....
   ....
   ....

   ii   eight 2 cm × 2 cm × 2 cm cubes

   ....
   ....
   ....
   ....
   ....

   iii   sixty-four 1 cm × 1 cm × 1 cm cubes

   ....
   ....

b   Explain the difference in surface area : volume ratio of the answers to part **a**.

   ....
   ....

Further questions

1   A student places a stick of chalk into a beaker then carefully pours in dilute hydrochloric acid until the chalk is completely covered. She then carefully breaks a second stick of chalk into four equal-sized pieces, places them in a new beaker and adds the same volume of acid.

   Each stick of chalk was 8 cm long with a diameter of 0.5 cm.

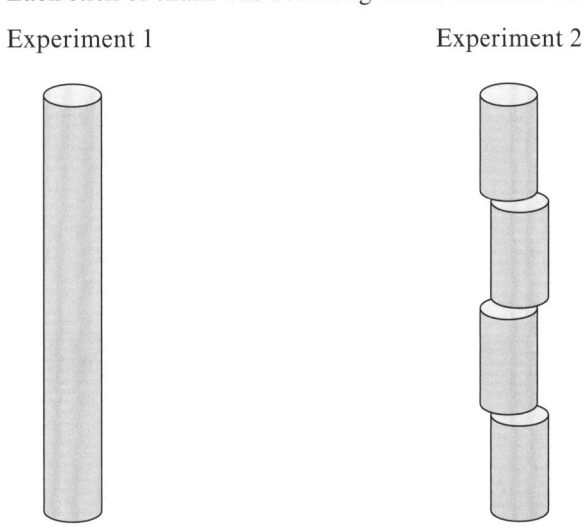

   Experiment 1   Experiment 2

Show mathematically why the reaction in the second experiment happened slightly more quickly than in the first.

....
....
....
....
....
....
....
....

2 Catalysts are used to increase the rate of reaction. In order to work, the catalyst must come into contact with the reactant. Some catalysts are layered onto another surface. The greater the surface area available, the more reactant can come into contact with the catalyst and the faster the reaction.

Some catalyst supports have a 3D honeycomb structure. If the block contained no honeycomb structure the catalyst would need to coat the inside faces of one large rectangular block. Instead the catalyst coats the inside of each hexagonal tube in the structure. Gases pass though these hexagonal tubes allowing the catalyst to catalyse any reactions.

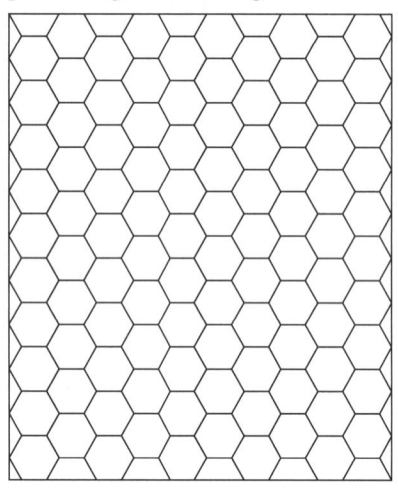

Figure 6.4 This honeycomb structure is coated with a catalyst, which can interact with gases as they pass though

Each hexagonal tube has sides of length 0.5 cm and the length of the tube is 25 cm.

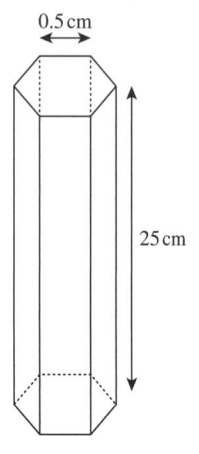

Figure 6.5 One hexagonal tube of the honeycomb structure

a   Calculate the surface area inside one hexagonal tube.

   ....

b   The block contains 100 hexagonal tubes. Calculate the total surface area inside the block.

   ....

c   The top of the block is a 10 cm × 10 cm square. Calculate the volume of the block.

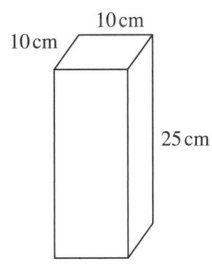

Figure 6.6 The dimensions of the block

   ....

d   Calculate the surface area : volume ratio of the block.

   ....

e   Compare the surface area : volume ratio of the block containing a honeycomb structure to that of a hollow block, 10 cm × 10 cm × 25 cm.

   ....
   ....

several maths skills

All exam-style questions and sample answers in this title were written by the authors.

In examinations, the way marks are awarded may be different.

1 Marble is made of the compound calcium carbonate. It reacts with hydrochloric acid producing carbon dioxide gas.

calcium carbonate + hydrochloric acid → calcium chloride + water + carbon dioxide

$$CaCO_3(s) + 2HCl(aq) \rightarrow CaCl_2(aq) + H_2O(l) + CO_2(g)$$

   a Use the relative atomic masses listed below to calculate the relative formula mass of

   i calcium carbonate

   ....

   ii carbon dioxide

   ....

	Relative atomic mass
Ca	40
C	12
O	16

   b Work out how many grams of carbon dioxide will be produced with these starting quantities of calcium carbonate.

   i 100 g

   ....

   ii 10 g

   ....

   iii 5 g

   ....

   c A student measures the total mass of some marble chips (calcium carbonate) and a flask containing hydrochloric acid.

   She then adds the marble chips to the flask and measures the total mass every minute.

   The mass gradually decreases as carbon dioxide gas is released.

   Calculate the loss of mass after each minute of the reaction. Record your answers in the table below.

   Loss of mass at a given time = mass at the start − mass at that time

Time	Total mass g	Loss of mass g
0 (Start)	79.4	
1	78.9	
2	78.3	
3	78.2	
4	77.7	
5	77.5	
6	77.5	

d Use the axes below to plot a graph to show the loss of mass over time.

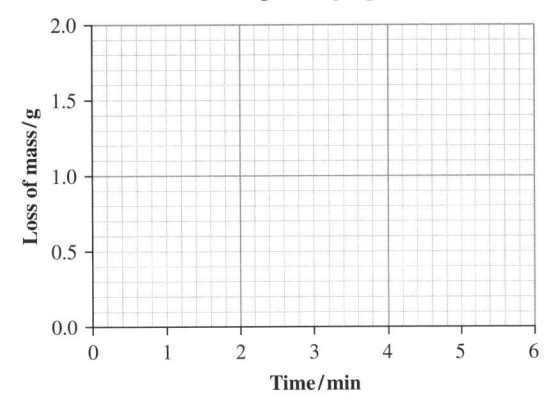

[Graph with y-axis "Loss of mass/g" from 0.0 to 2.0 and x-axis "Time/min" from 0 to 6]

e Look at the shape of the graph.

  i Name the feature of the graph that shows the rate of reaction.

  ....

  ii Describe how the rate of reaction changes.

  ....

  ....

  ....

  iii Use the graph to work out approximately when the reaction stopped.

  ....

  ....

  ....

2 Vinegar is a solution of ethanoic acid in water. A student carried out an experiment to find the concentration of ethanoic acid in a sample from a bottle of vinegar.

First the student added 25.0 cm³ of vinegar to a conical flask and added a few drops of indicator.

Next, she gradually added sodium hydroxide from a burette to the flask until the vinegar was exactly neutralised. She then carried out the experiment two more times.

a Use the burette diagrams to record the volumes of sodium hydroxide added from the burette.

Experiment	Burette diagram	Volume of sodium hydroxide added /cm³
1	(meniscus at 22.1)	
2	(meniscus at 22.2)	
3	(meniscus at 22.3)	

b Calculate the mean volume of sodium hydroxide added.

....

c The concentration of the sodium hydroxide was known to be 1 mol/dm³.

   i Rearrange the formula below so that moles is on the left-hand side.

   $$\text{concentration} = \frac{\text{moles}}{\text{volume (in dm}^3\text{)}}$$

   moles =

   ii Use the rearranged formula to calculate the number of moles of sodium hydroxide that were added from the burette. The concentration of sodium hydroxide was 1 mol/dm³.

   Number of moles of sodium hydroxide = ...

   ....

   ....

   ....

d The chemical equation for the reaction between ethanoic acid and sodium hydroxide is shown below:

$$CH_3COOH(aq) + NaOH(aq) \rightarrow CH_3COONa(aq) + H_2O(l)$$

  i Use the chemical equation for the reaction to work out how many moles of ethanoic acid react with 1 mole of sodium hydroxide.

  ....

  ii Write down the number of moles of ethanoic acid that reacted with the sodium hydroxide.

  ....

e Calculate the concentration of ethanoic acid in the sample.

....

....

....

Cambridge IGCSE Chemistry Maths Skills

The Periodic Table

I	II												III	IV	V	VI	VII	VIII/0
																		2 **He** Helium 4
3 **Li** Lithium 7	4 **Be** Beryllium 9												5 **B** Boron 11	6 **C** Carbon 12	7 **N** Nitrogen 14	8 **O** Oxygen 16	9 **F** Fluorine 19	10 **Ne** Neon 20
11 **Na** Sodium 23	12 **Mg** Magnesium 24												13 **Al** Aluminium 27	14 **Si** Silicon 28	15 **P** Phosphorus 31	16 **S** Sulfur 32	17 **Cl** Chlorine 35.5	18 **Ar** Argon 40
19 **K** Potassium 39	20 **Ca** Calcium 40	21 **Sc** Scandium 45	22 **Ti** Titanium 48	23 **V** Vanadium 51	24 **Cr** Chromium 52	25 **Mn** Manganese 55	26 **Fe** Iron 56	27 **Co** Cobalt 59	28 **Ni** Nickel 59	29 **Cu** Copper 64	30 **Zn** Zinc 65		31 **Ga** Gallium 70	32 **Ge** Germanium 73	33 **As** Arsenic 75	34 **Se** Selenium 79	35 **Br** Bromine 80	36 **Kr** Krypton 84
37 **Rb** Rubidium 85	38 **Sr** Strontium 88	39 **Y** Yttrium 89	40 **Zr** Zirconium 91	41 **Nb** Niobium 93	42 **Mo** Molybdenum 96	43 **Tc** Technetium –	44 **Ru** Ruthenium 101	45 **Rh** Rhodium 103	46 **Pd** Palladium 106	47 **Ag** Silver 108	48 **Cd** Cadmium 112		49 **In** Indium 115	50 **Sn** Tin 119	51 **Sb** Antimony 122	52 **Te** Tellurium 128	53 **I** Iodine 127	54 **Xe** Xenon 131
55 **Cs** Caesium 133	56 **Ba** Barium 137	57 * **La** Lanthanum 139	72 **Hf** Hafnium 179	73 **Ta** Tantalum 181	74 **W** Tungsten 184	75 **Re** Rhenium 186	76 **Os** Osmium 190	77 **Ir** Iridium 192	78 **Pt** Platinum 195	79 **Au** Gold 197	80 **Hg** Mercury 201		81 **Tl** Thallium 204	82 **Pb** Lead 207	83 **Bi** Bismuth 209	84 **Po** Polonium 209	85 **At** Astatine 210	86 **Rn** Radon 222
87 **Fr** Francium 223	88 **Ra** Radium 226	89 † **Ac** Actinium 227	104 **Rf** Rutherfordium 261	105 **Db** Dubnium 262	106 **Sg** Seaborgium 263	107 **Bh** Bohrium 264	108 **Hs** Hassium 265	109 **Mt** Meitnerium 268	110 **Ds** Darmstadtium 281	111 **Rg** Roentgenium 273	112 **Cn** Copernicium –		113 **Uut** Ununtrium –	114 **Fl** Flerovium –	115 **Uup** Ununpentium –	116 **Lv** Livermorium –	117 **Uus** Ununseptium –	118 **Uuo** Ununoctium –

Key:
a = atomic number
X = atomic symbol
b = relative atomic mass

*58–71 Lanthanoid series

58 **Ce** Cerium 140	59 **Pr** Praseodymium 141	60 **Nd** Neodymium 144	61 **Pm** Promethium 145	62 **Sm** Samarium 150	63 **Eu** Europium 152	64 **Gd** Gadolinium 157	65 **Tb** Terbium 159	66 **Dy** Dysprosium 163	67 **Ho** Holmium 165	68 **Er** Erbium 167	69 **Tm** Thulium 169	70 **Yb** Ytterbium 173	71 **Lu** Lutetium 175

†90–103 Actinoid series

90 **Th** Thorium 232	91 **Pa** Protactinium 231	92 **U** Uranium 238	93 **Np** Neptunium 237	94 **Pu** Plutonium 244	95 **Am** Americium 243	96 **Cm** Curium 247	97 **Bk** Berkelium 247	98 **Cf** Californium 251	99 **Es** Einsteinium 252	100 **Fm** Fermium 257	101 **Md** Mendelevium 258	102 **No** Nobelium 259	103 **Lr** Lawrencium 262

Group

1
H
Hydrogen
1

Glossary

accuracy How close a value is to the true value

angle A measure of the amount of turn between two adjoining or intersecting lines; this may be determined, in degrees, using a protractor

anomalous result One of a series of repeated experimental results that is much larger or smaller than the others

area A measure of the size of a surface (measured in square units, for example cm^2 or m^2)

axis A reference line on a graph or chart, along which a distance scale represents values of a variable

bar chart A chart with separated rectangular bars of equal width; the height (or length) of a bar represents the value of the variable

best-fit line A straight line or a smooth curve drawn on a graph that passes through or close to as many as possible of the data points; it represents the best estimate of the relationship between the variables.

BIDMAS 'Brackets, Indices, Division/Multiplication, Addition/Subtraction)', which is the order in which mathematical operations are done in a multi-step calculation

categorical data Data that can be grouped into categories (types) but not ordered

circumference The distance around a circle

continuous data Data that can take any numerical value within a range

control variable Variable that is kept constant in an investigation

coordinates Values that determine the position of a data point on a graph, relative to the axes

decimal place The place-value position of a number after a decimal point; the number 6.357 has three decimal places

dependent variable The variable that is measured or observed in an investigation, when the independent variable is changed

diameter A straight line connecting two points on a circle (or sphere) that passes through the centre

directly proportional The relationship between two variables such that when one doubles, the other doubles; the graph of the two variables is a straight line through the origin

discrete data Data that can take only certain values

equation A mathematical statement, using an equals sign, showing that two expressions are equal

estimate (Find) an approximate value

extrapolate Extending the line of best fit on a graph beyond the range of the data, in order to estimate values not within the data set

formula An equation that shows the relationship between variables

gradient The slope (steepness) of a line on a graph; it is calculated by dividing the vertical change by the horizontal change

independent variable Variable in an investigation that is changed by the experimenter

index A small raised number that indicates the power; for example, the index 4 here shows that the 2 is raised to the power 4, which means four 2s multiplied together:

$$2^4 = 2 \times 2 \times 2 \times 2$$

intercept The point at which a line on a graph crosses one of the axes; usually refers to the intercept with the vertical axis

interpolate On a graph, to estimate the value of a variable from the value of the other variable, using a best-fit line; on a scale, to estimate a measurement that falls between two scale marks

intersect Where two lines on a graph meet or cross one another

inverse sine The $\sin^{-1}$ function: the angle whose sine has a given value; for example if $\sin \theta = \frac{1}{2}$, then $\theta = \sin^{-1} \frac{1}{2} = 30°$

inversely proportional The relationship between two variables such that when one doubles, the other halves

line graph A graph of one variable against another where the data points fall on or close to a single line, which may be straight, curved, or straight-line segments between points, depending on the relationship between the variables

linear relationship A relationship between two variables that can be represented on a graph by a straight line

magnitude The size of something

mean An average value: the sum of a set of values divided by the number of values in the set

meniscus The curved surface of a liquid in a tube or cylinder

negative relationship When one variable decreases as the other increases

order of magnitude Approximate size of a number, often given as a power of 10; for example, the order of magnitude of 2700 is 10^3

origin The point on a graph at which the value of both variables is zero and where the axes cross

outlier A value in a data set, or point on a graph, that is considered unusual compared with the trend of other values

parallelogram A four-sided figure with two pairs of equal opposite sides, which are parallel

percentage A fraction expressed out of 100, e.g. $\frac{1}{2} = \frac{50}{100} = 50\%$

perpendicular At 90° to, or at right angles to

pie chart A circular chart that is divided into sectors which represent the relative values of components: the angle of the sector is proportional to the value of the component

positive relationship When one variable increases as the other increases

power A number raised to the power 2 is squared (e.g. x^2); a number raised to the power 3 is cubed (e.g. x^3); and so on

power of ten A number such as 10^3 or 10^{-3}

precise Close agreement between several measured values obtained by repeated measurements. The precision of a single value can be indicated by the number of significant figures given in the number; for example 4.027 has greater precision (is more precise) than 4.0

processed data Data produced by calculation using raw experimental data

product The result of multiplying two or more values

qualitative data Data that are descriptive and not numerical

quantitative data Data that are numerical

radius The distance from the centre of a circle (or sphere) to the circle (or sphere surface)

random error Measurement error that varies in an unpredictable way from one measurement to the next

range The interval between a lowest value and a highest value, for example of a measured variable or on the scale of a measuring instrument

rate A measure of how much one variable changes relative to another variable; usually how quickly a variable changes as time progresses

ratio A comparison of two numbers or of two measurements with the same unit; the ratio of A to B can be written $A:B$ or expressed as a fraction $\frac{A}{B}$

raw data Data collected by measurement or observation

rearrange To manipulate an equation mathematically so that the unknown value can be calculated; also termed 'change the subject'

reciprocal 1 divided by a value; for example the reciprocal of A is $\frac{1}{A}$

resolution The smallest change in a value that can be observed on a measuring instrument

rounding Expressing a number as an approximation, with fewer significant figures, for example, 7.436 rounded to two significant figure is 7.4, or rounded to three significant figures it is 7.44

scalar A variable that has size (magnitude) only

scale A set of marks with equal intervals, for example on a graph axis or a measuring cylinder;

or, on a scale diagram, the ratio of a length in the diagram to the actual size

scale diagram A diagram in which all lengths are in the same ratio to the corresponding lengths in the actual object (to the same scale)

scientific notation Another term for standard form

significant figures The number of digits in a number, not including any zeros at the beginning; for example the number of significant figures in 0.0682 is three

sine Mathematical function of an angle, abbreviated to sin

standard form Notation in which a number is written as a number between 1 and 10 multiplied by a power of 10; for example 4.78×10^9; also called **scientific notation** or **standard index form**

standard index form Another term for **standard form**

surface area The total area of surface of a three-dimensional object

systematic error Measurement error that results when measured values differ from the true value by the same amount each time a measurement is made; this may occur, for example, when a balance reads 0.02 g with no mass on it

trend A pattern shown by data; on a graph this may be shown by points following a 'trend line', the best estimate of this being the best-fit line

uncertainty Range of variation in experimental results because of sources of error; the true value is expected to be within this range

unit A standard used in measuring a variable, for example the metre or the volt

unit prefix A prefix (term added to the front of a word) added to a unit name to indicate a power of 10 of that unit, e.g. 1 millimetre = 10^{-3} metre

vector A variable that has a magnitude (size) and a direction

volume A measure of three-dimensional space (measured in cubic units e.g. cm^3 or m^3)

Acknowledgements

The authors and publishers acknowledge the following sources of copyright material and are grateful for the permissions granted.

Thanks to the following for permission to reproduce images:

Cover David Taylor/Science Photo Library; *Inside* Martyn F. Chillmaid/Science Photo Library; Sputnik/Science Photo Library.